Daily Devotions
from a
Preacher's Wife

by
Katie OBrian

January

*H*appy New Year! This is the traditional greeting today. Someone will say, "I hope you have a happy and prosperous New Year". Being prosperous does not make a person happy. We might be blessed with all the material things we want and more and there will be a void in our lives if we do not know Jesus Christ. Knowing Jesus Christ as Savior and Lord gives us the incentive to work for our physical daily needs.

The Book of Proverbs tells us to consider the ant and we know it works continuously, but material things, when put first, will not make us happy. Jesus will supply us all our needs and these are not just physical needs but the heart-felt need of love and security. That security is knowing we are in His arms and He is always there for us. He never sleeps or slumbers. He tells us to come to him if we are heavy laden (troubled) and He will give us rest.

So, during the coming year, let us place all our cares on Jesus, knowing He cares for us and He will give us peace and happiness in this life and a home in Heaven.

Read: John 4:10-14

When we are high above the earth gazing down from an airplane everything looks so small. Let us think of looking at the things when we are on the ground. The trees dwarf us and the rivers do not look like ribbons, anymore. Now, let us think of the problems we have in this life. Sometimes we feel dwarfed and discouraged, not knowing what we should do or how we should do it.

We feel walled in and helpless by things we have no control over. But let us look at these problems from Heaven, from God's prospective. He sees the opportunities for us to trust Him and He waits to lift those problems from us and take them into His large Hands. He will take them and make them bearable for His children. We know that, with God, our problems can be overcome. Ask your heavenly Burden-bearer for His prospective today and see that this is your opportunity to draw closer to Him.

Read: 2nd Corinthians 4:6-10

Corrie Ten Boon wrote "The Hiding Place", a book about the terror of prison camps for the Jewish people in Germany, and in this book she made this statement: "we gathered around the Bible holding out our hearts to its warmth and light". She also made a statement we should pay close attention to. "The blacker the night, the brighter and truer burned the Word of God." This was a witness given by a woman who was inside a Nazi prison camp. There was one Bible that was smuggled and preserved and she read aloud to the other women.

God spoke to these women He made it possible for them to read and hear His Word. He will give each of us the same joy if we will only read and meditate on His Word. The Bible is God talking to us and Prayer is the way we talk to God. At this moment God is wanting to speak to you and me. He reveals His great Love in the Bible and He wants to tell us about it. When circumstances seem black, do not give up, do not despair. In the pages of God's Holy Word is the light and warmth like a blazing fire. Let the Word of God warm you, guide you, and bring you light in the darkness.

Read: Psalm 119:105

*H*ave you ever thought of asking God to uncrowd your mind? We get so busy with thoughts of so many other things. For instance, where will I go?, What will I do in my time away from work? Will I do this or that? We find our minds and hearts so full of the things of this world, we do not think of God and His blessings. Looking at our thoughts, what should come first? "Lord, help me to stay silent until Your still small voice speaks to me." "Help me to think on Your Word until the understanding I am seeking becomes clear." "Help me to listen to others who have pain and remember you are the great Physican, and pray for them". "Give me the knowledge to know, except for the Grace of God there go I." "Help me to clear my life of clutter and pride. and depend totally on You."

Really praying to God is not using great words or depending on seeing miracles. We just need to free the mind so God will take up residence, there. Elijah saw a lot of God's great power, but He heard God speak to him in a quiet whisper. In stillness our hearts open and our minds surrender to Him.

Read: 1st Kings 19:11-13

$\mathcal{T}$he earthly life is a battle. A person will say, "if it isn't one thing, one sorrow, it is another". God never promised we would have a life of ease. We look at John The Baptist and see how he paved the way for Jesus. He was a great man and did his work for God, but this did not keep him from losing his life on earth, being killed by an evil person. Was God in it? When I look at this happening I see that John was used by God to serve Him until his work on earth was done.

When our work for God on earth is done, then God will allow us to die and take us to Himself in heaven. When we have troubles and heartaches on earth, let us remember we have a Father in heaven and He is in control and when our work is completed, time for us will be no more, because we will live with Him eternally. We each need to look at this new year and determine to do the work God has called us to do. The first step is yielding to the will of God.

Read: 1st Peter 1:3-7

*T*here is a song that begins with a question, "are you weary, are you broken hearted?" and then the answer is next, "tell it to Jesus". We know He is a Friend who sticketh closer than a brother and He understands all our troubles and fears. We are not to allow ourselves to grow bitter because of trouble. If we do this, Satan is very pleased, because He will then cause us to take our eyes off Jesus and dwell on the bitterness and troubles we have. In other words, if Satan could help us put our minds on ourselves and our families, only, we would think of nothing else.

We could become very selfish human beings, praying only for me and mine. As we cope with this world, let us see further than the pain of today, but the eternal picture God has given us in His Word. Sometimes it is hard to see the eternal prospective but we know this life isn't all there is, so tell it to Jesus alone. He is waiting to commune with you.

Read: 2nd Corinthians 4:6-10

During this extremely cold weather we think, "oh, I would just love to wrap up in a comforter in front of a blazing fire with a cup of something hot". This is comfort. We are obligated to learn how to live well and live a full life as opposed to thinking of the comfortable life. When God provides us with times of comfort, we are to thank Him, realizing He is the giver of all good gifts.

When times are hard and not so comfortable, we need to think of God teaching us to live life fully. He has more for us in life than just to be comfortable. He may call us to tasks that we do not want to do and do not enjoy, He wants us to give some of our time to serve Him, and we might have to face troubles that are so very hard to bear. Through it all we will learn to trust in Jesus, we will learn to trust His Word and above all Jesus will teach us to depend on Him, to live life to the fullest. Let us pray that Jesus will use each of us in this New Year, in His service and help us put Him first.

Read: John 10:7, 9 & 10

*F*or a long time I have heard this: "sticks and stones may break my bones, but words can never hurt me". WRONG We have heard many things in our lives that are totally wrong and when we study God's Word we see the errors. When in anger, frustration, or trouble we say hurtful things to others, we must remember after the words are out of our mouth, they cannot be taken back. We might ask forgiveness and feel very sorry for having said these things, but the hurt or hurts have been hurled at someone.

Most of the time the angry words are voiced to the ones we love the most. We can damage our testimony and damage the life of someone else by our tongues. So, words can hurt each of us. Years ago, I remember a person in the church being so damaged by gossip that he killed himself, because he felt people would never forgive him. Ask the Heavenly Father to help you be compassionate, kind, considerate and loving to those you come in contact with daily, Helping us control our tongues.

Read: James 1:26, 2:3-6

*A*fter a person encounters or we say meets God, that person should be changed. We can talk all day about our experiences and put on all kinds of show, but all this will amount to nothing if we do not "walk what we talk". Our everyday life is the testimony other people see. Those we live with, work with, talk to each day are seeing our true lives.

We cannot have an encounter with God and walk away the same person. He loves us enough to confront us when we have jealously, pride, unforgiveness, and other besetting problems. He is the only one who can change us from the inside and out. He will reveal His truth in love and as we listen, think, and learn we will grow as a Christian should. This encounter with Jesus Christ is more than a good story to tell, it will cause us to live differently, loving others with Christian love and knowing we are loved by the Heavenly Father. This is the joy unspeakable.

Read: 1st John 1:5-7 and 2: 15-17

$\mathcal{D}$o you go to the house of the Lord to worship each week? What does worship mean to you? We have some scriptures that tell us that everything is to be done decently and in order. We are to consider our fellow Christians at all times and not hinder their time with the Lord. When I am in a congregation, worship is not just about me but all those around me.

People have come because they have different needs. There are many who need encouragement and I pray that God will help me be a person to lift up my brothers and sisters. The Pastor has worked hard to prepare the sermon God has for us. Let us not keep others from hearing and consecrating on the message he brings. I would like to go home thinking about the message and God's Word and what He was saying to me this week. Let us be loving, considerate, sincere, and worship the Lord in Spirit and Truth.

Read: 1st Corinthians 14:40 &33; 13:25-27

*W*hen we are young we have great dreams of everything beautiful. We have our parents to provide for us and we are protected, but as we grow up we learn that evil is real. The attacks from Satan can come from any direction, blindsiding us. We are tempted on every side, because Satan cannot rest if a person is serving God. When we become lazy, he is busy. Satan has many weapons to use against us. Sometimes the weapons are fear and worry. We cannot run and pretend these things do not exist, because in our weakest moments they are before us.

Are we willing to do battle for Christ? Are we willing do battle against the darkness? We are not left to our own devises, but have to depend upon God's power and wear the armor He provides When we dress in this armor, we can go out and help take back ground from Satan, help bring light into our world. Dress in your armor, you are needed on the battlefield.

Read: Ephesians 6:11-17 and don't forget to pray.

*W*hen troubles, sickness and hardship comes what keeps us going? There is one thing that keeps us going and that is faith. Faith enables us to take the next step when we are ill and we need the motivation to move forward, our faith will sustain us.

When we trust in Jesus, our perseverance is born of the faith we have in Him. Our physical strength might run out and we want to give up, because our own strength,- determination, and dreams will not keep us going. Look in God's Word, faith is the One who calmed the raging sea, healed the sick, raised the dead and gave sight to the blind.

Faith in that One will keeps us showing up and taking one more step. Whatever God calls us to do, He will provide strength and the energy to do it. No matter how tired you are take that next step, depending on Jesus, and He will help you to persevere.

Read: Isaiah 40:30 & 31

Open my eyes, Lord, that I might see. I am not talking about seeing in the physical sense, but I desire to see spiritually. This is from Helen Keller, who was blind: "But how shall I speak of the glories I have discovered in the Bible? I have read it with an ever-broadening sense of joy and inspiration; and I love it as I love no other book."

When you open your Bible and run your hand over its pages imagine reading the way Helen did. It contains love letters from God. This is a treasure chest, filled with love, instructions and history, given to us by God inspiring different writers to pen the words we find there. This is like a special delivery letter sent to us through many servants of God.

Let us not take God's Word to us lightly, but realize He wants us to read it, asking for understanding, and the wisdom of God's Love in each word to us. The Bible is a special gift, be thankful for the privilege of using it!

Read: Psalm 119:105 & Romans 15:4

*I*t is a great, wonderful truth that all our happiness temporal, spiritual and eternal depend on us giving ourselves to God. We should think of God, our loving Father lifting us and carrying us just like an earthly parent carries their child to the best and safest place and protects them. God, just like an earthly parent wants the best for His children, so it would be foolish to resist His care, to choose to live apart from Him.

Often our will moves away from Him, because we have a choice, and sometimes the grass looks greener on the other side of the fence, so to speak. When we stray, we will fall because sinful ways last only for a season. Jesus is waiting there to pick up the pieces of our lives that have fallen apart. He will forgive and put His loving arms around us, if we ask Him to do so.

God loves each of us completely and Jesus came to die for each person, but it is up to us to choose to serve, lean on Him, or reject Him and go our own way.

Read: Psalm 62:1 & 2 and Matthew 23:37

We have just finished the month of December and Christmas and we all had on our minds the things we wanted to give others. What about the rest of the year? We know gifts are meant to be given and a gift, wrapped in shiny paper, stored in the closet will bring no joy to anyone. The joy comes in giving and sharing. The ultimate gift we have been given is the forgiveness of Jesus. He is God's gift to a needy world.

There are many people who are needy, those we will see and those who are far away. Do we really care what is happening to others? We should enjoy giving to those we know and love and those we do not know, those who are ill, and those who are broken hearted and troubled. You might say, "what can I give?"

There are many who need prayer, encouragement, and to know someone is thinking of them. Do you pay attention to those with whom you come in contact each day? We will find no joy in selfishness and keeping what God has given us to ourselves. Again the question: "Do You Really Care?"

Read: Galatians 5:22 and Galatians 6:2

Sometimes we have to grit our teeth to refrain from saying something back to a person who is insulting us. Harsh words hit us like a fist and we, as Christians, know we are to do good for evil. It is very hard to smile in many circumstances, but with the grace of God, we can do it. What do we do with the hurt?

The answer is always the same, take it to Jesus because He is always there and He cares. We ask Him to give us the grace to pray for those who hurt us. Those who have inflicted pain on us may have suffered great hurts, themselves, and need our prayer.

Maybe God wants to reach that person through us. Are we willing to put our feelings aside and do good for evil? A loving reaction could soften a troubled, hardened heart. Let us pray that God will use each of us as we show forgiveness for others.

Read: Matthew 5:44-46

God does not intend us to live a life that is filled with turmoil and stress. We can tell by looking at His creation He is a God of order. Many times we do not pay attention to this, but go through the day at breakneck speed. We become frazzled, short tempered and frustrated. This pace does not please God and is not good for the human body.

If we will follow God's plan, we will be more productive and effective. When we follow this plan we might have to say no to an activity we would love to do and we might even disappoint someone. It is pleasing to God that we live in an orderly way. We look at the sky at night and see the beautiful warmth of stars and the moon and see God's handiwork, and everything is in order, warm and peaceful.

When we trust Him to help us plan our lives, we will find the same order, peace and warmth.

Read Psalm 8:3-5

I read a poem about waiting on the Lord. When asked for an answer to prayer He answered "wait". The person was impatient and wanted an answer immediately. They wanted God to say "yes" to their petition. They wanted to know why He did not answer at once and why they were in this ordeal. So the asking began, "Lord, is your hand shortened?" "Have you not heard my praying and weeping all night." "You told me to claim your word." "My future and the future my family hangs in the balance and you are telling me to wait." The person said, "God, you could give me a sign, because I know you can darken the heavens, and raise the dead." God answered, "My Child I could give you all that you ask, but you would not know me, you would not know the depth of my love, you would not see through the clouds of despair, you would not learn to trust and simply know I am here."

"You would not know what I mean when I say My Grace is sufficient for thee". I realize, as the person in this poem, one of the hardest things to is wait when we or our loved ones are having trouble and we are asking God to intervene. Is God giving us this trial to strengthen us and make us learn to depend on Him more?

Read: 2nd Corinthians 12:8-10

*W*hat is the secret to happiness? Sure, we face many times of trouble and discouragement, but we have an answer. Do we become unhappy, and out of sorts because things do not go our way. The song says "are you weary, heavy hearted? give it to Jesus." We, as Christians, are to be peaceful, and trusting in Jesus, keeping our eyes on Him day by day. In other words, we Christians are to be the happiest people in the world because we have so many blessings.

There will be eternal happiness in heaven after this life. This is the gift from Jesus, as He died on the cross. We are all sinful creatures, but Jesus loved us so much, He was willing to die so that we could go to heaven. He prayed, "Father, forgive them." Knowing we have been forgiven let us go through each day following the recipe for happiness given by Paul.

Read: Colossians 3:13-17

$\mathcal{F}$ailure is a sad word. We don't want to fail in anything, but our desire is to do the job we have started. Actually we fear failure. Success a great, but how do we measure success? Is it the amount of money in our bank account or the property we own, how popular or well known we are? God does not measure success the way we do, but He measures humility and hates pride. Pride in our accomplishments is dangerous. This is the thing that can render all our work and efforts useless to God.

The sin of pride will creep in slowly and the use of great gifts will mean nothing to God. When pride has taken her abode we find ourselves forging ahead without the guidance of God. To be useful to God we must live our lives depending on Him being in control and we must serve Him with humility and love, only for His glory, and not for the praise of man.

Read: Proverbs 11:2 and Luke 18:11-14

Do you have times you feel that God is far away? Does your faith need stirring? We know that Jesus is present because He has promised never to leave us or forsake us, but things are bad and we have prayed and prayed and do not see results. Then, as John did when he was in prison we ask, "do I need to look for another to help me?" "Lord, are you really there?"

We must remember God never moved away from us, but we have moved further from Him. We need to examine ourselves. "How long and how much have I prayed, lately?" "Have I studied God's Word and had a quiet time with Him during these busy days"? When we feel our faith growing weak we need to go to some of the old saints of the Bible. They did not have the material things we have today, but they had their weak moments just like we do.

We are to believe and follow Jesus without knowing the outcome of our actions. He just told His disciples to "follow me".

Read: Hebrews Chapter 11

*W*hen we think of perfection, what do we think of? Do we see a perfect holiday, a perfect body, or a perfect home? If we strive for perfection in these areas we will become very frustrated because there is always someone who will tell of a holiday that seems more perfect, a body more beautiful and we see a home that is much more perfect than ours. But what about our life?

The only way we can strive for perfection in our life is trusting Jesus each day we live. We will never reach that goal but we are to look forward to it. The day of perfection will be the day we go to heaven. All will be perfect there. Here, on earth, we are to strive for perfection by bringing light to a dark world. Jesus is the light and in heaven there will be no need for the sun because of the light of God. Everything will be perfect light and there will be no darkness at all.

Read: Revelation 22:1-7

Does every person have to deal with doubt during times we do not understand? Yes, even those who serve God. When God called Moses from the burning bush, he did not believe he was capable of delivering his people. He doubted God's Word that He would be with him.

When Gideon put a fleece before the Lord seeking direction and God answered, he doubted. He asked for the fleece the second time to be sure. The priest, Zacharias, questioned the angel who told him a son, John, was to be born. Even though Zacharias was serving God he thought of his age and the age of his wife and doubted.

The disciple, Philip asked Jesus to show them the Father and they would be satisfied. This happened just after Jesus gave them the most beautiful message, the most beautiful promise and we know when Jesus makes a promise, He will keep that promise, so let us not doubt but rely on God's Word.

Read: John 14:1-7

$\mathcal{A}$ quiet time with God is most precious for every Christian. We cannot always get away without interruptions. During our solitude the phone might ring or something else might interrupt. We are not to become discouraged, but find time when these interruptions will not be likely. The early morning hours are a great time to commune with God. Everyone else is sleeping, and all is quiet in your home. This is your time so rise, an hour earlier, and take advantage of the quiet. This can become a daily routine for each of us and we will get through our hectic days better.

Of course we all have demands on our time but we must remember God has given us the time and He does not demand anything in return. Do we love Him enough to set aside a period for Bible study and talking and listening to Him for His leadership? If, after all you are doing, does not give you the solitude you need, let God guide you. You can always be in a prayerful state, praying to yourself as you drive or pray as you go about your job through the day.

Read: Psalm 25:4-6

*E*very person has a choice in life. One person wrote of her captivity by terrorists for a long time. During this time she had no privacy, no conveniences, and was on the brink of starvation all the time. Even though mistreated so badly she realized she had a choice to make. She could harbor resentment and stay angry with those who had treated her so poorly and live the rest of her life hating or she could trust God , knowing even these circumstances were under His control and would make her a stronger Christian. Because of these hardships she would learn to depend on God more. She chose to trust God and live the rest of her life letting Him work in her life instead of bitterness.

The question is this: What is causing your hurt, bitterness and resentment? You, too, have a choice. You can give in to those feelings or you can trust God, believing His Word.

Read: John 17:13-17

*T*his morning I am thinking of the woman who had the issue of blood for twelve years. During this time she had to keep to herself, hoping the issue would stop soon. Let us put ourselves in her place. When she heard that Jesus was coming, she was determined to get to him somehow. She was ashamed to come to Jesus boldly because of her condition, so she had to creep up behind Him. She would have had her head covered and she would not want the other people to know her condition, because she could not help touching people as the pushed through the great crowd. We must remember the law of the Pharisees was that she should be shunned because she was unclean. They did not touch unclean things.

She knew Jesus, the Healer, would heal her if she could just get to touch His garment. When we are away from Jesus we keep our head low, because we do not want others to see our "spiritual anemia". Jesus invites us to come close. Just a touch from Him will heal us.

Read: Mark 5:25-34

*W*e all want a second chance when we "mess up". That is why Jesus died on the cross. Even though a person has been living a sinful life until now, they still have a chance to come to Jesus and accept Him. Even after that experience we mess up at times and have to go back to Him and ask forgiveness. We are always asking for a chance to do better.

One thing we must remember is this: though we go our own way and wander away from God at times, He will forgive us. There are people who say, "God want forgive me because I have been too mean". This isn't true. Do you think anyone has been meaner than Saul who was having Christians dragged out and beaten, put in prison to stop them from believing in Jesus? Yet, God forgave him and he became one of the great preachers of the gospel in the New Testament and suffered many things for Christ.

When we read the Bible we see that no-one is good and Jesus will forgive all the same, if they come to Him.

Read: Acts 8:1-3

*T*he fundamental part of our perseverance is Faith. Many times it is tough to keep going, and we feel that our strength is gone. When our body is sick and we are feeling weakened, and we are tired in mind and limb, what will motivate us to keep going? There is only one reason and that reason is Jesus.

Our faith in Him will last when everything else runs out. Our own determination, desires and dreams may not be enough but Jesus, the one who calmed the sea, raised the dead, healed the sick, restored sight to the blind should be our reason for taking one more step.

Whatever you have been called to do and no matter what happens in your life, remember this: faith will preserve you and it will sustain you as you take the next step.

Read: Isaiah 40:30 & 31

How do we think of God's Word? Do we think of it as something we need to read because it is on our "to do" list? Sometimes we forget that God's Words are not merely words but words to be ingested. We can read words all day and not take them into our hearts. We can read in a hurry, with other things on our mind, and never think of that precious Scripture during the rest of the day. If we are reading God's Word for head knowledge, only, we will come away empty and unfulfilled. We need to fully engage our hearts.

The Bible is the most beautiful Book ever written. God had men to write as He inspired and gave them the messages and these messages are for every phase of our lives. God knew His prize creation would rebel and fail to obey Him. He also knew how many sorrows life would hold for those who loved Him. The Bible tells us about healing, faith, love, worship, and warning us about the wiles of Satan and the havoc he can play with our lives.

So, we have history of others and their failures, and the love of an almighty God in the pages of God's Word. Read it, think on it, love it, and obey it.

Read: Psalm 40:1-8

1 know I write about peace a lot, but this is very important to me. I want to live in a quiet, peaceful home without turmoil and Jesus is the one that will help us hold our tongue and keep things peaceful. Even though we want outward peace there is one kind of peace that goes deep, that penetrates the very soul of a person.

Only Jesus can bring that kind of peace because He gives us peace that passes understanding and does not go away. Jesus' peace will never change. What are you facing today?

Is your world less than peaceful? All the promises Jesus made are forever and He has promised to give us peace and to give it freely. Turn to Him and let this peace wash over you today and walk in peace.

Read: John 14:26 & 27

*H*iding from God is rebellion. When we hide from God, we are saying we don't want to hear from Him. Is this because we, as Adam & Eve, do not want to face our sin but rather live with it?

We can hide from God by staying busy, We might be doing good things, but not God's things. The truth is we think we are hiding from God but this is impossible. He knows where we are. Let's not hide, but ask Him to show us how He wants us to live each day. Come to the light and love of Jesus who died so that we can have eternal salvation.

Read: Psalm 40:1-5

February

There is a wide-spread teaching that a person will never have a problem if they trust Jesus. In my words it is said that everything would be perfect. Not true! God never promised us we would not have problems in this life. He never said we would be excused from the storms and have only sunshine. Yes, a perfect place is being prepared for those who have trusted Jesus as Savior, but we will attain this perfection only after death.

Heaven is more beautiful than we can imagine and Jesus said, "I go to prepare a place for you." Let us remember those who teach in error and lead people to believe God will heal after ordering a prayer cloth or sending money are false prophets. The Bible never teaches that God makes everything glorious on this earth. It does teach we have the Holy Spirit as our Comforter and that Jesus will walk with us through the trials of life. God does answer prayer, but not always suddenly will we get a yes. Some people are only healed after death when they obtain the perfect body.

We must remember Jesus cares for each of us and He hears our prayers and petitions, but we should always pray that His Will be done.

Read: John 16:20-22 and John 16:33

When we read one of the most beautiful of Jesus' sermons, The Beatitudes, we see how much we fail Him many times. He says do not judge and do not look at the mote (small speck) in your brothers eye, but behold the beam in your own eye. How easy it is to see the fault of another, especially of someone who has ways and attitudes we do not like. If we like a person, we will most likely overlook the same fault and excuse them. Also, when we look at forgiveness there are some Scriptures that are hard for us to do.

Are we a big enough Christians to do good for evil? Can we bless a person who curses us? When a person does us wrong do we remember that Jesus said "vengeance is mine, I will repay" or do we try to revenge ourselves? My prayer today is this: "Lord, help me to become more like you". "Help me to lay all these feelings and burdens at your feet, always."

Read: John 6:27-30

*I*f a person takes offence easily, and we call this wearing a chip on your shoulder, they will live in unfriendliness and will know nothing of Calvary's Love. When we, as Christians forget about God's love for us, our feelings get hurt easily. When we look for others offences and sins and this becomes our focus, we have lost our correct focus. Our attention should be on God and what He has done for us.

We must remember we did not deserve His forgiveness. If a person has accepted the forgiveness of Christ and than refuses to forgive others, they know nothing of the love of Jesus Christ. When our cups become full of the forgiveness of Christ, we can overflow that unconditional love to others.

Let us enjoy the Love Jesus has given so freely and spread it around.

Read: Ephesians 4:30-32

Did you wake up with thankfulness on your mind, this morning? God has given us so much to be thankful for. You might say, "well He didn't take this headache away" or "He has not solved my problem, yet." Did you have a comfortable bed in which to sleep and food to eat? Do you have clothes in which to dress yourself? Have you stopped to count your blessings, lately?

What about the grace of a loving God who made a way that we could have salvation and live with Him forever? Remember the Scripture tells us the Lord is good, His Mercy is everlasting and His Truth endureth to all generations.

How long has it been since you thanked God for the freedom to read His precious Word, to go to His house and worship?

Read: Psalm 37:3-9

*A*n infant has no choice in the matter of surrender. A loving parent lifts the child and carries it, providing what is best for it. How foolish we are to resist the loving Father, and insist on living apart from Him when He has a deep love for us that is beyond our imagination. The great truth is wonderful and undeniable, that all our happiness: temporal, spiritual and eternal consists in one thing and that one thing is resigning ourselves to God, and leaving ourselves with Him. God loves each of us deeply and fully and wants to give us abiding joy that is full and lasting.

How do I surrender to this loving God? Accept Him as Savior and Lord, let Him enfold you and carry you in His loving Arms. He is waiting for you to come to Him.

Read: Psalm 62:1 & 2

*J*ust like a cluttered workshop, our hearts and souls can become cluttered with the things of the world that are not pleasing to God. There are many different kinds of clutter that will take up the space. There is desire for wealth, prestige, and an accumulation of stuff, or a craving to be noticed and appreciated by others leaving Christ out of it.

We need to let Jesus in to do His work. In other words we need a spiritual housecleaning and to clean house is to let go of all these things that will hinder us from worshiping and serving Jesus Christ. Let each of us invite Jesus into our workshop, our life, because we need Him to help us clean it up. He is the Master Craftsman and He has a plan for more beautiful than any one of us can imagine.

Stop, Look, and Listen! See what He is working on in you today!

Read: John 3:16

*A*re we alert to the people we meet each day? Do we remember that the Bible tells us we could entertain angels unaware? When we depend upon the Lord's leadership, there will be many opportunities to talk to others, to help others, the encourage those to whom we are able to show Christian kindness.

It is sad that we live in a world that so many are far from God and people are afraid of each other. As we go down the road and see a person walking, we are afraid to stop to lend a hand. We have read the stories of many who did this and were murdered for their effort to be of help. How sad that Satan has such a hold on our Nation and officials that corruption has become the norm and young people, growing up in this day are afraid to trust others.

At one time two people could make a promise and shake hands on it, but now everything has to be signed and dated. God help us to come back to Him as a Nation that will not condone criminal behavior and Christians will sincerely trust in Him once more. Christians, we need to Pray!

Read: Jeremiah 33:2 & 3

God loves you and me, but there is no favorites with Him. He died for each person in the world, rich or poor and He saw only souls in need of redemption. When I say redemption, I think of a slave that owes a huge fine and has nothing to pay. Jesus came to buy us out of slavery with His Lifeblood. The Pharisees thought they were above others, special, and there are people today who think they are God's favorites.

The disciples gave us examples of this. James and John ask for the highest seats in Christ's kingdom. How sad this must have made Jesus because He was seeing the selfishness of His disciples. We find Paul rebuking Peter for shunning Gentiles when the Jews came from Jerusalem. Before the Jews came Peter was fellowshipping with the Gentiles, but when these people arrived he did not eat with them. Are we just like Peter was?

Do we think ourselves to be more religious, better than others. We are all saved by the Grace of God and we can do nothing to buy this wonderful gift, it is freely given. Jesus showed us He loved all people unconditionally and we are not saved any other way except by faith in Jesus Christ and He knows the heart.

Read: Galatians 2:11-14

*I*s your life like the person who builds his house on the sand? Is there foundation in the way you believe? Do you listen to God's word and then turn it off and go your merry way, never thinking on it again? Jesus said if we do not listen and do the things He says, we are like a man who builds a house that will fall with trouble. Of course He is saying that our faith should be well grounded to live in this world and trust Him when we have trouble and sorrow.

To have well-grounded faith is like a man who prepared his ground, digging deep because the foundation is the main part of the building. Trusting Jesus, giving Him our lives is the preparation that is most important. If there is pretending going on the faith will be shallow and fail in time of trouble.

Read: Luke 6:47-49

How do we react to God's Love for us? Can we, like Fannie Crosby refuse to weep and sigh because we are having a hard time in this life, or are we determined to lift others up? If we are not content, we will take offence easily. Inside we are troubled and angry and this makes us angry with everyone else. We then, become unfriendly with those around us. If we continue in this cold unfriendliness we know nothing of Calvary's Love.

When we get our feelings hurt easily, we forget we have a Friend that will stick closer to us than a brother. We forget Jesus loved us so much He was willing to die so that we could inherit eternal life. When we have accepted Calvary'sLove, our cups will be so full they will overflow to others. Fannie Crosby is one of my hero's of the faith. Even though she was blind, she let God use her by writing beautiful hymns to lift others up and show them the love of God.

Read: Psalm 18:1-3

What a wonderful day God has given us! Do you feel the excitement when you think you might meet someone you will be able to help, today? Did you know God puts people in our pathway? We do not know how much a kind word, a smile and a little conversation might help someone, might lift them up today. Many people out there are hurting and many feel hopeless.

We, as Christians, have a chance to bring sunshine and hope into someone's life. But, you might answer, "I am all grumpy and out of sorts this morning, and don't feel like smiling, laughing or even talking to anyone. "What is the answer? Have you prayed to God, asking Him to lift you up and keep you through the day? Have you given Him your troubles and left them with Him?

Have you thanked Him for saving you so that you will have eternal life in a beautiful heavenly home that is beyond our imagination? Jesus is there, waiting to listen to your prayer and to lift you up. Talk to Him! Stop thinking of yourself and see the needs of others.

Read: 1st Thessalonians 5:14-18

*H*ow many times do we hear a sermon from God's Word and go directly from the place of worship forgetting the message God had for us? I look at the parable of the sower and see the seed, the Word of God, sown in different soils or we might say different hearts. Jesus gave the meaning of the parable and the first seeds explained are the ones that a person who is interested in God's Word, and Satan comes and put other things into the heart, keeping the one interested from trusting Jesus.

He explained the seed that fell on the rock had no root system and just like any plant we know, it will stay alive only for a short time. We think of the ones that fell among the thorns. Do we let the cares of this life stifle us and keep us from serving God? When the seed is planted on good ground they will become plants and grow becoming fruitful.

Read: Luke 7:10-15

*W*hen you look in the mirror, do you hurry because you know you will be disappointed? Do we have a perfect picture in mind and wish we looked like that? What you are seeing is only the outer shell. The person you are inside is the real you and God looks upon His children as beautiful. He sees them covered with the blood of Jesus.

So, it isn't necessary to God to try to tighten up the wrinkles in our faces, or make ourselves into a different person outside. Sure, He has given us this body to nourish and keep clean and as healthy as possible for as long as possible, but to be honest, kind, patient, loving, giving and living our lives for Jesus Christ is the most important. If we belong to Jesus, we have the responsibility to let our lives shine during this one life we have been given.

We are to let others see Him in us. There is a song we have heard that says, "I was made to serve the Lord". So, when we look in the mirror today, let us each remember that the Lord is looking upon the inside, and thank Him for His goodness to each of us.

Read: 1st John 1:7

*H*ave a great Valentine's Day! When we think of Valentine's day we think of love. Each human being wants to be loved by others. This is s natural trait of everyone.

I can tell you of a Love that is much greater than any human can give and that is the Love of Jesus Christ. We read that "God is Love" and we know this is true. We say we love others but we would not give our child to hang on the cross for others. When we are ill, we need the love and support of our family and friends and this means so much to us.

When the time comes for us to die, if we belong to the heavenly Father, His love will sustain. I read of Stephen and hear him, as he is transferred to heaven saying, "I see heavens open and I see the Son of man, Jesus, standing on the right hand of God". We know that Scripture teaches us Jesus was seated on God's right hand. Love caused Him to stand and receive Stephen.

Read: 1st Corinthians 13:13 & remember charity is love.

*T*hinking of time this morning. We are so very aware of our appointments and the time we have to do this or that. What about the time God has allotted us. I think of John the Baptist and see that when his work was finished he went to be with the Lord.

So it is with each Christian. We do not need to waste the precious time God has given us, but use it to serve and glorify God. I have heard it said that no matter the years of your life, you can look back to childhood and the time seems very short. We think, "where did the time go"?

God does not see time as we do, even though He knows all about the years we have, but a thousand years is but a day with Him. In His timetable this would mean Jesus has been gone a short time. What will I be able to do for Jesus this weekend? Lord, please help me to be a witness in word and deed.

Read: 2nd Peter 3:8 & 9

*D*o we want to put God in a box of our choosing and say, "If things aren't good, God is not with us?" There is a song I have been thinking of since hearing it last night.

He is God on the mountain and He is also God in the Valley. He is God of the day and also God of the night. When we have trouble we do not understand why. We might say, "But God I have served you to the best of my ability and I do not know why this is happening to me". I think we have all been in this situation. Jesus did not promise we would not have trouble in this life, but He promised to be with us during the troubled times.

We must remember we now look into a glass darkly. You will find this in First Corinthians 13:12. In other words we do not see the picture clearly, but God knows everything that is going on in each life. Let us trust Him for everything.

Read: Jeremiah 29:11 & 12

What if God appeared to you and asked you what you desire He give you? What would you request from God? Would we be so greedy for this world's goods we would ask for wealth or political power?

Solomon looked back to the blessings he has gotten before this and realized he was as a little child, totally dependent upon God. He showed his humbleness by telling God he did not know what to do. Even though he was king, now, he realized he was helpless without God. Solomon asked for an understanding heart so that he could wisely judge the people and this was pleasing to God. Actually, he was asking for wisdom which only God can give.

This should be our prayer when we read the Bible. "Lord, give me an understanding heart on your Word. Help me to know what You are saying to me and the meaning of all Your teachings." We can gather knowledge from the written word, but only God can give us the wisdom to know His will.

Read: Proverbs 9: 10-12 & Proverbs 8:11

*W*hen we invite Jesus in, we should give Him room for His workshop. When we think of a workshop we know there are tools involved and these tools are used for making and molding. We need to clean a space of all the clutter of desire for wealth, and the desire for popularity, and always wanting to be noticed. When we give Jesus the space He needs to work on us, spiritual house-cleaning needs to be done.

That is the process of freeing ourselves from these worldly attachments. Did you know that Jesus will willingly help you clean all this up and make you anew, because He is the Master Craftsman. His plan for you is more beautiful than you can imagine.

Read: 1st John 2:15-17

Who should a Christian have for a best friend? We should associate with people who are walking in the right way. When I say the right way, I am saying people who strive to live as close to God as possible. People who are honest, straight forward and who have strong Christian principles. If these are the people we associate with, they have the ability to make you and me want to walk closer to God.

When you need advise about a problem to whom do you go? Do you go to a person with these Christian principles or do you go to a person that believes in nothing? A Christian can walk alongside another Christian because the two agree. Their wisdom is true, because it is gleaned from walking with God.

Christian, we need each other to make our way through this life because we know if troubles do not face us now, we will have troubled times in the future. Each mountain has a valley. When we trust God to help us through each time, He is a present help in trouble.

Read: Amos 3:3 & 8:11 Let us pray for our country.

*T*he anchor of a great ship is small compared to the size of the great ship, yet when dropped on the ocean floor it holds the ship in place. We have an anchor for our souls and that is faith in God and it holds us safe. When circumstances in this life make no sense to us and we have questions with no answers, faith means we know God sees the big picture.

What about the stormy times when our troubles have grown so large, faith means we know that God will not fail us. Each of us will go through testing times in our life, and it is during these times we grow stronger because we learn to depend upon the only One who has the answers. Jesus is the One who is always present in times of trouble.

Do not anchor your soul on the appearance of things but on who God is. He is able to hold us steady in this life, so may we each keep on serving Him, because no matter what, God is still God, and as the song says, "The Anchor holds in spite of the storm."

Read: 2nd Corinthians 5:6-9

We were made for a perfect world and God's creation was perfect until the work of Satan entered into it. So, instead of a life of perfection, this is a life of love and pain. You cannot have love without pain, because with the consolations of love there is tinges of grief, misunderstanding and loss. Even though we have pain in this life, it can lead us to a pathway to understanding love.

We hear people say, "I love material things, this and that" and that isn't real love. Real love is the kind of love God has for us. True love calls for giving and must endure sacrifice and forgiveness. Jesus is the one who showed the perfect love when He sacrificed His life for us on the cross. He was willing to do whatever it took to bring us to Himself. Are we willing to sacrifice for someone we love? Do we think, "this is not best for me"? Do we have the thought of me, me, me all day without considering another's feelings? Jesus never put Himself first and we are to follow His example.

Read: 1st John 3:16 & 17

Life is a journey. We are born into the world knowing nothing and the rest of life is a learning process. When we know we are to make a journey, we prepare for it. We pack clothes, and make sure all the things around home are taken care of. What about the journey of life? God says He knows His plans for us, plans to do us good.

Jeremiah 29:11. Are we willing to follow those plans? We have choices throughout the years, we are given to live. You might say, "I have tried to follow God's plans and I have had much trouble and sorrow. I am almost ready to give up." When we come to a time like this let us remember we have a Helper and He is always there to offer guidance, comfort and peace. Because of Satan's ploys and falling short of God's standards, we were separated from Him, spiritually dead. But God provided a way for us to connect with Him by sending His Son to die for us for payment of this sin. Romans 3:23 tells us this and now we have help.

Read: Psalm 46:1

*L*et us all be aware of how others feel. When you say something to someone and they snap at you, how does this make you feel? This will happen to us from time to time and when it does, let us stop to realize that the person snapping at us might have had a bad time at home or troubles we know nothing about. Our first reaction is to snap back. This was the way of the Pharisees, "an eye for an eye" and tooth for a tooth". Always repaying evil for evil. This does not show the love of Christ in our lives.

As a follower you are a member of His Body. Each part of the body has a place and a job to do, just like the parts of our physical body. Others will know we belong to Jesus, are part of that Body of Christians, by the way we treat our fellow man. Others are watching you. Can they tell by your words and your actions that you are a Christian?

Read: John 13:34 & 35

Do we think God has given us a bare minimum of information? Do we think of the Scripture that tells us we look in a glass darkly, but then we will know, as was written in 1st Corinthians 13:12? We are a people who want to know all the answers, but God has given us all He would have us know. When we think on this, we realize we do not even take in all the information we have and use it as we should. We are not left in darkness because we have the Bible. In the beginning of the Bible God spoke light into the world. He expects us to ask for wisdom to understand the Words He has given us. Before we study God's Word we need to pray for wisdom to see the things He wants us to see and understand.

The Bible gives us all the direction we need, so why do we struggle to find our way? God is willing to direct us, but we often want to have things our way and we know God has given us a free will to choose the way we go. Do you ask wisdom from God everyday? When we ask for the wisdom of God to light our way, are we willing to follow that light? Do we think it too much sacrifice to serve Him? When we accept Jesus Christ as our Lord, we are no more a part of the world. The Scripture tells us we are in the world but not of the world. We become a new person, risen with Christ. We are joined with Christ now and hereafter.

Read: Colossians 3:1-4

We hear many ads about taking vitamins to help us feel younger, gives us energy, and help us live longer, but we never hear about the vitamin that gives us eternal life and that is Jesus Christ, who died so that we might inherit eternal life in Heaven.

Sure, I believe in taking vitamins and keeping the body as healthy as possible, because God gave me this body to nourish and care for. Are we guilty of taking care of our physical bodies and ignoring the spiritual body? How much time do we use in Prayer and Bible study each day? Are we guilty of waiting until the end of the day and then we remember we should talk to God? We get into bed and start to say, "now I lay me down to sleep" and drift off to sleep because we are so worn out with the cares of the day and the entertainment from TV, we just can't stay awake another minute. We are guilty of using our time for everything else, and leaving God out of the day. Let us be aware that Jesus is waiting. He wants to shepherd us, to commune with us, protect and lead us in our daily life.

Think of the old hymn Jesus Hold my hand, I need Thee every hour.

Read: Psalm 23

What has happened to us that we think of our wants as our needs? Children think they need a pair of shoes that have a name brand on them because someone else has these and they say, "I need these shoes". In a place like Tanzania and other areas of the world the children are living in cardboard boxes, not knowing where the next food will come from.

We, in America, have been so blessed, but we have become selfish, always thinking of what I want and even calling these wants needs. Some of us can remember when there was work for a child to do around the house and that kept us occupied. Even though we did not like it, the lifestyle we had made us stronger people. We learned we could not have everything we wanted.

God has blessed us so much and we forget that when times are not as good, we can tighten our belts, not having all our wants and still get along perfectly well. The greatest need in each life is knowing God and remembering how He blesses us each day. Our prayer should be, "Lord help me through this hard time and help me to respond to my circumstances in a way that will be pleasing to you."

Read: Philippians 4:6 & 7 and Verse 19

$\mathcal{T}$ he capacity to discern (know) the will of God comes through the study of His Word and communication with Him (Prayer). We should be alert to the all that God is telling us in His Word and humble enough to live by It. There is a ploy of Satan today that wants us to believe we cannot have a good time if we live by Christian standards. This is not true. The things God told us to stay away from are for our protection. For instance, if we keep the body clean, as the temple of the Holy Spirit, there will be no alcoholic, no addictions to drugs and other things that cause sickness and death. There will be no babies aborted or without parents. Because of rebellion and people wanting to live in their lifestyle instead of the one God has set forth, many have gone through life with much grief and heartache. God loves us and the Bible is written so that we might live happy lives in fellowship with Him. God spoke to Moses for the good of the people and Moses listened to Him. Maybe we do not hear the Voice of God, as Moses did, but He will lead us by the study of His Word and as we commune with Him each day.

Read: Exodus 33:11, 13 & 14

*L*ife is a series of happy times and sad times. We have sorrows and we have times of great joy. Our greatest joy should be in the fact that we have a relationship with God. He gives us the great gift of holding us up when we lean on him in times of sorrow, in times when problems seem to overwhelm us. He sees the big picture of our lives. He knows the trials that will make us strong and He is there when we become weak. Oh, what a Savior and what gifts He gives! We have the tendency of thinking God should insulate us from problems, but this is not the realities of life. God wants to see that our joy is not in worldly pleasures, but in our relationship with Him and in the realization of blessings He gives us.

Let us step out of the difficulties for a short time and look into the Face of our Heavenly Father who loves us so much. This is the love that really matters in this life. Remember the song tells us that the Love of God, how rich and pure and it shall forever more endure. It is matchless and strong. Be determined, "no matter what happens in this life the Lord is my strength."

Read: Habakkuk 3:17-19

*T*here seems to be a growing trend of doing away with things called tradition. We have one tradition that has stayed with us. That is this day because of leap year. This occurs once each four years and adds a day to the calendar. Is this upsetting? No, because people expect it every four years.

Are changes upsetting to you? Do you think the deciplies were upset when they saw Jesus on the Mount with Moses and Elijah, who had been dead for hundreds of years? They saw Jesus changed from the one they looked upon a short time before. He was transfigured before them. In other words, he took on a glorified body.

It is most beautiful when we realize they knew who Jesus was talking with, even though they had never seen these two men.

Some changes are beautiful, but there is one thing that does not change and that is God's Word.

Read: Matthew 17:1-4

March

Sometimes we make bad decisions in our life. This decision was made without going to God and seeking His will for us. We can make a foolish decision and at times complex situations arise as the result. We then wonder how we are going to cope and how we will recover from the results of our actions.

We must remember, even though we got ourselves into a mess, God's grace still prevails. Sure, our actions have consequences and we hurt because of them, but God watches over His own. He leaves us to our choices, but when we leave Him out of our decisions and go our way, God watches over us and when we seek forgiveness, He will forgive and transform the situation into a greater purpose. We must never give up on ourselves, because God has not given up on any one of us. We have learned because of our mistakes and God will use the pain of recovery as a learning process, growing us into more mature Christians.

Read: Psalm 25:8-12

*A*s we go to worship, or if anyone is sick in bed and cannot go to worship, let us pray for our Country. We might think, "what can one person do?" The nation is made up of individuals and one by one we can make a difference. We think of the picture of one stone thrown into the water and the ripples are seen for a long distance.

God hears our prayer when we sincerely ask Him to intervene and bless our Nation, our homes and our Churches. The core of faith begins in the home and we should be very careful to live a lifestyle that our children and grandchildren will see and know we are praying for God to bless our Country and bless them in the future. Lord, help us each to remember our actions speak louder than words. Little eyes are watching and little ears are listening and ideas are developing.

Read: Philippians 4:5-8

*T*he song of Solomon speaks of little foxes that spoil the vine and the tender grapes. I look at this and think of the way different people grew up and the happenings in our lives. These things have molded our thinking to an extent. For instance, a person can take offense easily in some areas. Are we extra sensitive when a person is trying to make a point? Do we think this is bully behavior? Everyone has issues. We just need to take note of this

We are not to feel alone, but go to God's Word when we are searching ourselves. Barnabas and Paul had a disagreement and this caused them to part ways for awhile. Had Paul had a bad experience with someone turning away from God's work, before, which made him less compassionate? We do not know the answer, but we know they both continued to serve God. Let us remember forgiving the small stuff is very important. Let us not act like Mary when she went to Jesus to tattle about her sister. We have the opportunity, each day, to overreact, hold grudges and distance ourselves from someone. We are human and we will encounter offense or create offense. The fault can belong to someone else or to us. God is still working on each of us and we need to come clean about our behavior.

Read: Romans 12:2 and Acts 10:38-42

Why does our loving Father God allow His children to have trouble? This is a question we hear many times. Where was God when this or that happened? Is it hard for you to answer, "He was there all the time." Let us think about Job. He was very comfortable in his world with plenty of worldly good and a good family, sitting within the hedge God had around him. When bad things happen there are those who want to say, as Job's friends did, "you have sinned, you have done something that is hidden and God is punishing you". This is not true and the story of Job proves it.

He was an upright man who loved God, but let us remember he was comfortable in his life. Does God want us to step out of our comfort zone and serve Him? We see the story of a man who loved God and was loved by God, but there was a purpose behind all the terrible things that happened to him. He became an experienced person who now knew who God was, and this knowledge brought him to repentance. Then Job saw himself, he was self righteous and lacked humility.

Read: Job 42:5 & 6

Sometimes God prompts us to call this person or visit that person and we want to say, "lord, I am so busy, I have so much to do, but I will do it later". Then, something happens and it is too late to be of help to that individual. You see, God knows all those who need encouragement. He gives us chances to receive blessings that we ignore and of course we miss the blessings of being of help to someone. I read a story of a person who was prompted to call a lady who had lost her son. She could not forget the feeling. and finally called the person who she hardly knew. The conversation lasted for some time, because that lady needed to know someone cared and was willing to listen to her troubles and pray with her.

There are many ways we might serve the Lord, daily, and showing compassion and caring when someone has troubles is a way to serve God and others. When we listen to the prompting of the Holy Spirit and serve others, we get the greater blessings, because we will know we have done what we could to help.

Read: 2nd Corinthians 1:4

We should never be afraid to do the job God calls us to do. If He calls you, He will give you the strength to complete the work He has for you. Yes, after we surrender our lives to the Lord, we all have something to do, because each person is unique. God gives different abilities and talents. Let us think of some of the characters in the Bible. Mary did not say, "I am too young", Esther knew she could be killed, but she was brave enough to do the job, Deborah did not say, "I cannot be a woman judge".

We find Moses using excuses, telling God He could not speak well. But we hear God saying, "I made your mouth". Because of his excuses, God used his brother to speak for him. Let us each search ourselves today. What is my excuse and what is your excuse for not serving God as we should. Let us look at the vision and message from God to Isaiah.

Read: Isaiah 6:5-8

$\mathcal{A}$s I was thinking and looking through my Bible I thought of the people who become so angry when someone is just trying to state their opinion. We all have issues and one of those for me is this: I do not like to see someone making fun of or bullying another. This could be a problem with me because some people raise their voice when they are just trying to make a point that is important to them. You might have something else that makes you angry.

We have many opportunities to make us over react, and as in the Song of Solomon we read that little foxes will spoil the vine. In other words, a little thing can grow into something big if we dwell on it. We find Martha going to Jesus with a minor thing. She tattled on her sister and wanted Jesus to scold her and instead Jesus told her Mary was doing the most important.

We also find Paul and Barnabas had a disagreement, so when we read about these people in the Bible, we know we are only human, also. God is not pleased when we become angry.

Read: Acts 15:36-41 and then Romans 12:1 & 2

I have always loved books and as a child I loved the stories that had happy endings. We all like to see good triumph over evil. The world thinks of happy endings as one bumper sticker states "visualize world peace", or "he who dies with the most toys, wins." These happy endings are never found, because in this life things happen that we do not expect and the joy of the moment is taken away and replaced by sadness.

We have another version of happy endings and that is God's version. Jesus came to earth, grew up and died so that we could have this happy ending. I am talking about eternal life that has been given by the shedding of the precious Blood of Jesus Christ. He went willingly to the cross for you and for me. When we accept Jesus Christ as our Savior and Lord, we will go to a perfect place, when this life is over, and we will see our Savior face to face. That is a happy ending!

Read: Rev. 22:4 & 5

Do we tend to come to God because we want something or do we honestly want to be with Him, love Him, adore Him? When we come to Him, knowing that He loved us so much He left Heaven and came to earth to live and endure the persecution of man and then die for us, we are showing our faith and love for Him.

When we accept Jesus and the Love He has shown for us, the Holy Spirit will come and live within us and will guide us in the ways we should go. Then, you might ask," why do I fail to follow the path I should go?" The answer to that is rebellion. We decide we want to do things our way and leave God out of our lives and refuse to listen to the Holy Spirit. You see, Jesus never leaves a person, but the person chooses to leave Him. He is there awaiting your return.

Hebrews 13:5 & Psalm 32:8-17

*L*et us think on truth today. Do you hate being told an untruth? You have depended on something this or that person has told you and find that it isn't truth at all. There has been deception since the beginning of time and this is sin. When we look at the story of Jacob and Esau in the Book of Genesis, we find the mother leaving God out and telling her husband a lie. Truth means we can count on it. As believers we count on God's Word knowing it is truth. We defend it, believe it and embrace it, but there is one more thing we must do.

We must walk in it, daily. This is not always easy but it is vital. We have found the truth that can change the world, changes lives, and changes hearts. May that truth effect every step we take today and every day. Everything God has said will stand.

Read: Psalm 86:11 & 12

*W*hat kind of friends do you have? Did you ever think of friendship being a vital part of your relationship with God? Some friends will pull you down to lower standards that are not in tune with the Word of God. Some will pull you toward God by their walk each day. There are some true friends in God's Word that were willing to tear off a roof to get their friend to Jesus.

There are those who will influence our dreams, some mentor us, and some connect us to other important relationships. Let us beware of friends who can send us in wrong directions. If we look around we will see many lives have been ruined because of bad influences. We need to discern those friends who would pull us down and set them aside. On the other hand, let us thank God for good friends. We should pray for them, encourage them and love and care for them because they are a gift from God.

Read: Mark 2:2-4

We live in a hurting world. If you need proof of this, visit a hospital and observe the suffering all around. Of course, we do not want to do this, but there are those who question, "Why does God allow this suffering to happen?" God lays down physical laws and if we do not observe these laws we suffer the consequence. Sometimes amid this suffering He will work a miracle and a person is well again. At other times he or she is not made better.

Sometimes it is just the time for this person or that person to go home to be with the Father. Their work on earth is finished. What is our responsibility to those who are hurting? We know it is to pray for them, help and give to them, maintaining an unwavering faith that will be a witness to others.

God knows the future for each person and we should always pray that His will be done in each life. Let us remember we are His hands and His feet in this world. Our touch, our words, and our prayers will bring God into our hurting world. Remember we are saved by faith and that faith will produce works.

Read: James 2:15-17

$\mathcal{D}$id you ever think of God's Word (the Bible) as a meal? I have been thinking of a very old hymn this morning and it is "Come and Dine". Most of you have probably never heard it, but it says "Jesus has a table spread where the saints of God are fed and invites His people to come and dine." We study God's Word and take it into ourselves, digest it, and it is food for our souls. We are to be hungry for God's Word, or I should say we should have a desire to know what it says.

No matter how much we study it, we will find something new each time we open the Bible. You might read a novel and tell it word for word, but the Bible is written so you cannot do this. Oh, yes we might memorize it, but then go back and think on the same verse and know that it is telling you something you have not seen in it before. Paul tells Timothy to study to show himself approved unto God, and this Scripture tells us that study is important to rightly divide the Word of Truth.

Let us be diligent with our Bible Study, asking God to open our understanding, always.

Read: 2nd Timothy 3:16 & 17

Satan is called the father of lies and this is very true. When he opened a cozy chat with Eve he used a deliberate lie, misquoting God. We very easily fall for lies. We hear of a cream that will make us younger, we waste our money ordering and trying it just to be disappointed. We hear of a way to quick wealth and we fall for it.

When the TV is turned on, we will hear many things that are lies. Satan knows where we are most vulnerable and he uses our weakness. He is looking for ways to get us off track spiritually and even sometimes quotes God's Word just enough to make us believe the lie. He wants to come between a Christian and God and will use any means to do so. If we listen to him, we lose. Have you not heard he just wants to get a small opening, a foot in the door? He will work gradually to get a person away from doing God's will. You might ask, "how will I be able to fight such a cunning force?" Our best defense is God's Word. Study it, talk about it, read it over and over to understand it, and know the truth is in God's Word, which He will gladly reveal to you if you ask Him.

Read: Psalm 119:103-105

*T*here are many times in our lives when we will say, "that's too hard for me." When we see a challenge that we think is too hard it is very easy to give up, to quit. God is not pleased with us when we give up and think we are not up to the task without going to Him in prayer about it.

A loving God permits hard things to come into our lives because the hard things bring us greater victories. When God told Gideon to eliminate a large portion of his army, I am sure Gideon thought it would be too hard to defeat the enemy with so few men. When the victory was won, he knew it was God who won it. Do you have something in your life that you think is impossible? Have you given it to God? When Jesus was scourged, beaten and treated in such an awful way and then hanged on a cross, was this not hard? Let us look beyond the task and see the resurrection! Look to Jesus to help each of us through the hard things in this life and when this life is over we are winners!

Read: Isaiah 61:3 and then read: Psalm 125:1 & 2

*D*o you have an early morning prayer? We should wake up each day and say, "Lord, I'm giving you full control of this day and all that concerns me. Do we go to God and worship Him or do we go to Him with petitions? When everything is going well, do we forget to thank Him? Too often we ignore our prayer life until we have trouble and then we petition God. Let us ask our heavenly Father to take blessed control of all our circumstances.

Remember "He is God in the good times and He is also God in the bad times." If we are on the mountain or in the valley, He is there. God lovingly calls us to trust Him alone. Fall back into His loving arms, He will catch you every time!

Read: Psalm 139:23 & 24

*D*o you want to see the Face of God? We need to observe and we will see His face in different places. What about the homeless person who is dirty and hungry. Jesus fed the hungry and we see Him here. We see a frowning Boss, giving his workers a hard time and wonder if we can see Jesus here. Yes, Jesus faced accusers who made unreasonable demands and was even crucified by them. Yet He said, "Father forgive them."

Is it possible to see God in sickness and pain? Yes, God's word teaches us that when we suffer, Jesus suffers. We see Him weeping with Mary and Martha, who were sorrowful because Lazarus had died. If we prayerfully look we will be able to see Jesus everywhere. Do we understand situations? No, but we must trust in Jesus and ask His will to be done. May we remember we can see Jesus in every person.

Read: James 2:1 & 8 & 9

*L*et us imagine how our days would be if we had our cups filled first thing in the morning. I am not talking about coffee, but our hearts as we go to God in a devotion each day. The alarm rings and we awake fuzzy with sleep, jumping from bed we begin to think of all the things we have to do this day. Sometimes the list seems so long we feel just like returning to bed for a few more hours of sleep, and just not face all the tasks before us. But everything is different if we go to God first thing each morning.

He will give His love, His peace, and His joy. Jesus wants to help us through the day, He is waiting for us to talk with Him. He knows just what we will need in the hours ahead.

Read: Psalm 5:1-3

Some thoughts posted on church signs that are worth thinking about: Seven days without prayer makes one weak; The devil is not afraid of a Bible with dust on it; The wages of sin will not be lowered; God is always on time; Give the devil an inch and he will become your ruler; Difficult times will either make us better or bitter; Prayer is the oil that takes the friction out of life; and the last one is my favorite. A person never stands as tall as when kneeling before God.

Does anyone remember the song that was sung by the quartets a long time ago, "On your knees you are taller than trees, yes taller, taller than trees" God is waiting to hear from each of us. Let us be ever conscious of our time with Him. I have seen bibles left on Church pews for the week and the owner will pick it up next Sunday. God talks to us through His word and we talk to Him through prayer. The disciples desired to pray and asked Jesus to teach them and we have the model prayer.

Read: Matthew 6:9-15

When things in our lives are broken, confused and we see nothing but hopelessness we need nothing short of a miracle. Yes, I believe in miracles and in a case like this something out of the ordinary has to happen. When this occurs relationships will be restored, emotions are steadied and minds are healed. We see something good comes from our brokenness. We are a stronger Christian, more dependent on God, realizing His goodness toward us.

God wants all of us and sometimes it takes brokenness for us to fully turn to Him. He doesn't want to be a "fair weather" friend. He wants to walk with us each day. Yes, miracles happen every day. Look around you and you will see them everywhere. A great miracle Is recorded in Acts when people of different nations heard and understood each other.

Read: Acts; 2:5-12

γou feel as though something is missing. You have accepted Jesus Christ as Savior and Lord, and you attend church regularly, yet there is an emptyspot inside. You feel the love of family and Christian friends, but something is lacking. If you listen closely you will hear sweet soft words from Jesus as He urges you to come closer. He wants His people to come close to Him, to feel the warmth of His presence. He wants to have a relationship with you and have you get to know Him more.

As you come to know Him, more deeply, you will experience the deep love He has for you. You will begin to walk with Him and talk with Him and the empty space within will disappear, because it has been filled with the Love of God.

Read: Ephesians 3:1 & 2 and Ephesians 1:17

There was a letter supposedly from God a few years ago and it showed the heartbreak He feels because of our unconcern.

The first thing the letter said was "I watched you wake up, and I hoped you would talk to me, thank me for blessings, or ask my leadership for the day, but you were looking for the right outfit to wear to work." "So I waited and you were busy for a time, running around the house doing many things". "You had to wait on your ride to work for fifteen minutes and, but you used that time on the telephone", "I watched as you went to work and waited all day and when you ate lunch, you did not say a word to me". "You went home and did a number of things and after watching TV for a time, finally fell into bed and went to sleep immediately". When we look at this, are we guilty of leaving God out of our day? The one who loves us so much, blesses us and waits patiently for us to talk to Him?

Read Psalm 119:1-7

Spring is here and we see everything come to life that appeared dead during the winter months. How beautiful to see a tree white with blooms! I look at these things and feel that God is giving us a picture of the resurrection each year. We look into God's Word and see Jesus in the Book of Luke as He took the three disciples with Him and we see Him transfigured, to me this is an angelic form, before their eyes, talking with Moses and Elijah. We must remember Moses and Elijah had been dead for a very long time and here they were, talking with Christ. What a picture!

Yes, we see Jesus as He arises from the tomb. We are given the picture of the resurrection many times. We will die, depart this life, only to be raised to a new life, if we belong to Jesus. When a Christian dies, we have to realize this is not the end, but only the beginning for him or her. Look around you and see things come to life that you thought were dead a few days ago, and realize what Jesus has done for you.

Read: 1st Thessalonians 4:13-18

*W*e need guidance each day. When we arise in the morning, we do not know what the day will hold for us. We might have a happy visit, a sad happening or the day could be ordinary with nothing happening that is special. We need the guidance of God to help up with anything we might encounter. Let us ask Him to lead us, to guide us and give us the wisdom to make right decisions. Jesus modeled how to recognize human limits and ask for divine direction. We find Him in the Garden of Gethsemane, praying to God because He knew what He must face.

When we are troubled, uncertain or confused, we are invited to go to a loving Father for guidance. He wants to guide us. He knows the future and He knows what we need. If we ask Him, He will replace our bewilderment with good sense and our troubled hearts with peace. Let God take your hand and lead you. This guidance from Him is personal and it is yours, Just ask.

Read: Psalm 107:6, Psalm and Psalm 48:14

*I*t is not enough to pray for answers, if we have our minds made up and are too stubborn to listen to what God is telling us. We have God's Word and there are many times when we say by our actions, "I don't care if it is in the Bible, I want to do it this way." We would not say this aloud, but actions speak louder than words. We have made up our minds and we do not want to change.

We think we know how God should deal with that person who has hurt us. We think we know how He should provide for us and when He should provide it. Sometimes God sends someone else to talk with us, to soften our hearts, in order to humble us and make us willing to do His Will, not ours. Study God's Word with an open heart and listen to what He is saying to you. His answers might surprise you!

Read: John 10:27 & 28

*T*he Love of Jesus is deeper than the deepest sea, and wider than the widest heavens. If we allow Jesus to enfold us in His arms we are safe, but we must invite Him in. He will not intrude and He stands at the door waiting for the invitation to come in and abide with each person. He will keep us from the darkness of Satan, if we depend on Him. In other words Jesus is the only one who can protect us from the storms of life.

No life is without stormy times and we can lean on Him to see us through those times. We can call out to Him and He will hear. We are never alone if we have His love...if we belong to Him, we are His beloved. He promises never to let us go.

Read: Romans 8:35-39

*D*o you know why God gives us a reason to put on armor? He gives each Christian weapons with which to fight evil. Yes, evil is real and Satan is real. He has resisted God from the beginning. He persuaded Eve and Adam followed. He knew God had given the human a choice to serve Him or to turn away from Him. That is why he finds a person's weaknesses and works on his or her thoughts, first. When the human thinks on something for a time and has neglected to study God's Word and Prayer asking for guidance, he or she is weak spiritually and will give in to Satan.

God does not leave us to our own devices, but gives us the power to fight Satan. Put on your Armor and get ready to do battle for God! The older Christians knew all about this battle and that is the reason they would sing a song, "Keep on the firing line."

Read: Ephesians 6:13-17 & verse 18 and "pray always"

*T*here are many times when we are in doubt and do not know which way to turn. At a time like this, do we sometimes forget to submit our judgment to the Will and Spirit of God? We can pray for Him to shut every door but the right one, and He will do so, because He has promised to supply our needs according to His riches in Glory. You will find this Scripture in Philippians 4: 19.

We might be in the process of trying to choose between more than one good option, but God will show you the best choice. If we submit to His Will and pray earnestly for the knowledge to know right choices, He will show us the door we should enter. Are we willing to patiently wait and submit to God's Will and Leadership?

Read: Acts: 16:6-10

*H*istory tells us when the great titanic began to sink the song was, "Nearer My God To Thee". Even though a person says he or she does not believe there is a God, when the time comes and they know they have only a few minutes left, I believe everyone is conscious they are going to see God. We do not need to wait until those moments to seek the nearness of God.

We may have His nearness and enjoy His presence each day of our lives if we only ask. His nearness will bring us peace and safety. Jesus went to the Cross so we could have this wonderful gift. Let us think like this: " a young child reaching for his or her mother's hand, nearness to God means He will reach down and clasp our hand." When we accept Jesus Christ and reach out to God we can always sing, "Nearer My God To Thee" and He will be there.

Read: James 4:8

*O*ur relationship with Jesus has to be an individual thing. No other person can accept Him as Savior and Lord for you. That is the reason Jesus asked the question of His disciples, in Luke, "Who do people say that I am?' The answer from the disciples was, some say John the Baptist, some say Elijah or another old prophet and then Jesus asked the most important question for any one of us to answer, "Who do YOU say I am?"

There are those who say a child has to be twelve years old to accept Jesus, this is not true. The idea comes from Jesus talking to the teachers and doctors of religion at the age of twelve. They were amazed at His knowledge. Study God's Word for yourself and do not listen to these man-made ideas. We believe a person may accept him at any age. Believing Him to be the Son of God is the only way to Heaven.

Read: Luke 9:18-21 and Luke 2:42, 46 & 47

*W*ere you disappointed recently because someone hurt you? Did you expect a loved one to visit and he or she did not come? These things happen in life. People who you love dearly desert you and tell you things that are not true. When this happens, you will be lonely and feel dejected and unloved. This is not true because there is one that loves at all times and that is Jesus Christ. As a Christian, never feel unloved, just turn to Jesus and talk to Him, telling Him all about the troubles you are having Jesus understands our every thought, and our hurts.

When Lazarus died his sisters were disappointed because Jesus had not come to keep this from happening. Do you think they became stronger believers when Jesus called Him forth from the tomb? When we walk with Jesus, He will stick closer than a brother.

Read John 11:21 and then Read John 11:32

April

When we think of praying without ceasing as the Bible tells us to do, we wonder how we can do that. We have to go about our daily routine of work and taking care of household chores and our children, so how can I have time to pray without ceasing? There is no certain position a person has to be in to pray. We are thinking all the time, so we are able to have prayer on our mind as we drive, clean house, or do other things.

God knows our thoughts and He knows our prayers if they are aloud or silent. It is not hard to pray all the time. This means we should be in an attitude of talking with God, depending on Him in each situation. God may not always answer your prayer quickly and that is the reason we are to continue praying to Him. You might ask, "does He always answer?" Yes, the answer could be yes, later or no. God knows the best for us and He gives good to His children.

Read: 1st Thessalonians 5:15-17

Why do we sign our prayers off with "in the Name of Jesus"? Because the Name of Jesus allowed us access to God in the first place. We could not go to Him if we did not have the perfect one standing between. This came to pass when Jesus died on the cross, shedding His precious Blood for our sins, so that we could go directly to the Father. Sure, we ask others to pray for us, but we do not have to have an earthly priest, anymore, because we have direct access to the throne of God through Jesus Christ.

When we accepted Jesus as Savior and Lord of our lives we become joint- heirs with Jesus Christ. This makes God our Father, and allows us to go to Him with our petitions at any time. When we say, "in Jesus Name", we are saying, "God, your Son, Jesus introduced me to You, and He told me I could talk to You at any time calling You my Father". Have you prayed today? Come on, talk to God in Jesus' Name.

Read: Hebrews 4:14-16

We have all lost loved ones and we will have these times again in our life-time. The beautiful thing for a Christian is knowing the loved one has gone to be with Jesus. We think of dying as being a horrible experience, but this is not so if we belong to God. Let us think of Stephen. He was stoned to death because he preached Jesus to the people and as he was dying he saw Jesus standing awaiting him.

We look in God's Word and we see that Jesus is seated at the right hand of the Father God. Now we see Him caring so much that He stands to greet one of His own when he dies. I believe this tells us, if we belong to Him, we will see Jesus waiting for us in those last moments of our earthly life. When our soul leaves this earth, we will be with Him. How Beautiful Heaven Must Be! We must realize, even though we miss our loved ones, they would not come back and live with the pain and troubles of this world.

Read: Acts 2:34 & Acts 7:56-60

*W*e should think about disobeying God. Every time we choose our way instead of God's way, we are rebelling against the God of the universe.

How do I know I am rebelling? Did you look into God's Word for the instructions He gives us? Jesus came to die, to shed His Blood, so that we would have a chance to live close to God. Does this mean I will live a life of perfection after choosing Jesus? No, but it does mean we will live the very best we can and never disobey God in a time of rebellion or we might say the time when the Holy Spirit is telling us this or that is wrong and we say, "I will do as I please". "I will do it my way, no matter what the Bible teaches."

Jesus loves us so much that He was willing to give His life for us and we should always desire to be close to Him. He only wants good for you and me. The choice is up to the individual.

Read:1st Peter 2:21-24

*H*ow many times do we think of the "what ifs" in our lives? I was reading in "Touched by an E-Mail" and saw this ; "What if God couldn't take time to bless us today, because we couldn't take time to thank Him for His blessings yesterday or if He stopped leading us tomorrow, because we refused to follow Him, today?"

So many blessings are taken for granted by all of us. We grumble about a rainy day and if we did not have rain we would not have food. Sometimes we tend to grumble because the message God has given our Pastors are too long, but what if God took away the Bible and we had no guidance from Him? We, in America have been blessed more than any other nation and we have forgotten God, the giver of all good gifts.

Let us become more conscious of our Father which is in Heaven, thanking Him and walking according to His Word. You might say, "I don't know His Word" and the answer to this is: Study the Bible to show yourself approved unto God, a workman that does not need to be ashamed because he or she doesn't know.

Read: Prov. 4:13-19

*W*e have heard the word destitute many times and we know when a person is destitute he or she is to be pitied. What about the destitute places we find ourselves in? There are times when we do not know which way to go, and nothing makes sense to us. It could be loss of the job we have been in for a long time, or a wandering child, loss of a home, a death, friendship or divorce.

We have all been in this destitute place sometime in our lifetime. In this place, darkness descends, envelops and overwhelms us? Who do we turn to, where do we go? Who can possibly bring sense back to our world of confusion? We can only cry out to God for help, because only He can give us the wisdom and strength to move forward from this place and back into life. He is the one who can turn your world right side up again. He is there, Just call on Him.

Read: Psalm 40:1-3

*A*re you content where you are? I was reading about a person having many problems and he thought his burdens were so heavy he could not carry them. He fell upon his knees and prayed a long time asking God to remove the cross he was carrying and give him another. He thought any cross would be lighter than his. God answered his prayer and told him to place his cross in a room, which he did. God then told the young man to go into the room and choose the cross he wished to bear. As the young man entered the room he saw many crosses. They were different sizes and some of them very large. He looked into a corner and saw a small cross and told God that was the cross he wanted to bear. His answer was: "son that was the cross you placed in the room".

We need to learn to look around us when things seem harder than we can handle and see that there are others who have more troubles than we do. Let us go our way, asking God to help us handle anything that arises and thank Him for all the blessings we each have.

Read: Philippians 4:11 & 13

There are many things in this life we need to remember, but there are other things we need to forget. We need to remember the many blessings God has given us, but we need to forget the times of defeat. Forget the mistakes we have made in this life, but never forget the lessons we have learned, and forget about the days we have been lonely by remembering the beautiful smiles of friends. When we spend our time thinking about pleasing ourselves and forgetting others, we will not function as Jesus taught in His Word. He came as a servant, even washing the feet of His disciples, never thinking of Himself.

We quickly think of our wants and feelings, first, and this keeps us from ministering to others many times. I pray that each of us will strive to put ourselves in someone's place who is less fortunate, today. When you see a person with terrible sickness or disabilities, do you think, "God bless that person, because except for Your Grace, there go I?" Let each of us be willing to put others first and our lives will be this: God first, others next, and I will be last.

Read: John 10:11-15

*L*ife is filled with choices. It is as though I am going down a road and there is a fork in the road. I look this way and that and wish I knew which one to take. Well, there is a way we can know. We have a good Shepherd to lead us if we know Jesus. You see doors and wonder which you should go through, ask Jesus to close each door of opportunity for you except the right one. After praying to God for direction, do we have enough faith to follow through the door that is open to us.

Sometimes a choice is easy because we have the knowledge to know the better way, but there are times when we see more ways than one that could be good and then we are confused. God wants to show you the best choices. Call on Him, depend on Him, follow Him. God showed His prophets and preachers the places and the people He would have them serve.

Read: Acts 16:6-10

*L*ove does not flow along on the easy paths, spending itself only on the attractive. The fact is that God is Love and God knows each of His children. He knows when one is hurting, when one is discouraged, has children in trouble, and has an illness that the doctors say they can do nothing about. Jesus saw the bleeding woman, the leper, the little man in the tree, the blind, and people tormented by demons. He showed love to each of these in need.

We must remember that Jesus is the example we are to follow. We are to let God's creative love guide us and we will meet many people with needs in unexpected places. When we love as Jesus loved we will recognize hurt, sorrow, and frustration on the faces of others. Are we alert to the needs of those we might be able to encourage, to pray for? Jesus, by His example has commissioned us to take the love of God where it is most needed.

Read: John 15:10-12

*L*et us think of the people around us. Somebody needs you as a friend, to listen and talk to them. Somebody thinks you are a gift from God and wants to hold your hand, Somebody treasures your spirit and that same person is looking at your life. Somebody needs you to have faith in them and let them know you love and believe in them. Somebody is thankful for you and praying for you, wishing they could see you.

Think of your influence, daily, because you never know who is watching you, who has faith in you, who depends on you for encouragement, and you do not want to disappoint anyone. Be careful and walk your talk, because several somebodies may be watching you. Remember "A word aptly spoken is like apples of gold in pitchers of silver." Prov. 25:11

Read: Prov. 22:1

We are a people who, when settled in, are comfortable and want to stay there. This is usually about the place we live and the friends we have, the church we attend, and even the places we shop. We like to have a vacation once a year and then go home and resume our activities. God does not want His children to "settle in" and this is not the address, but the service He has for each of us.

Have you committed your life to Him? Have you asked Him what He would have you do today? Do you know of someone who needs an encouraging word? A helping hand? Are we each willing to get out of our comfort zone for the Glory of God? A person might say, "I am not able to go to different places, " You might only be able to mail cards, or make telephone calls to those who need to know someone cares. If we ask God, He will show us what He wants us to do. Let us not react like Moses, when God told him to go to Pharaoh. Moses made the excuse of not being able to speak and God would have given him that ability, had he obeyed immediately. Instead, God gave him Aaron to go with him. God wants each of us to catch a new vision of what He can do in and through us. He has great plans for you, Pray to Him. Call on Him.

Read: 1st Chronicles 4:10 & Exodus 4:10 & 11

You are a Christian, you have accepted Jesus Christ as your Savior and Lord, so why the negative thoughts? Are you afraid of what you might have to face? Do you know when a person worries about what could happen, he or she is missing the joys of the present. When we tend to worry about those things that could be in our future, we are showing no faith in Jesus Christ and the things we worry about will most likely never happen.

We, as Christians, should lift our heads and realize we have a wonderful God who will help us through every storm we might face. He knows all about us and will give us strength to face any thing we might encounter. We need to think of life as a journey and we are to grab the wheel and learn how to sail the ship with the help of Jesus. Are you facing choppy seas now? Does your ship seem to be taking on water? Remember the Captain, Jesus, is at the helm with you.

Read: Luke 8:23-25

Do you identify yourself with your job, parent of your children, or another ambition that has been fulfilled? If so, you stand to be disappointed because our circumstances change. We might lose our jobs, have a sudden illness and children move out leaving an empty nest. What will happen to your identity then? We need to place our identity in that which will never change and that is our Lord Jesus Christ. He is the same yesterday, today and forever.

When we identify with Jesus, we know we have a place to serve on this earth and we also know we have a heavenly home awaiting us for eternity. When you truly accept Him, you are His forever, no matter what changes are happens in your life today. Just come to Him, place your identity in Him. Remember conversation is daily living.

Read: Hebrews 13:5,6 & 8

Christianity is not confined to the Church and not to be exercised only in prayer and meditation. We are to attend worship, or we say go to church, because the Bible tells us not to forsake the assembling of ourselves together. We each need to know we have the prayers and support of others and Church attendance should enforce this.

If we are Christians, we have faith in Jesus Christ and it is not to be limited to the above mentioned things, but we are to show our faith in our everyday walk and talk. We will show our love for Christ by our acts of kindness, doing our jobs well as in giving a boss a days work for a days pay, and encouraging those who are grieving, and helping others. People who follow Christ are not to be silenced. Wherever we go and whatever we do, we are living our faith, and we know we are in the Lord's presence at all times.

Read: 1st Corinthians 10:31-33

*H*ave you prayed and prayed about something and nothing has happened and you think, My prayers are pointless". What are we to do when this time comes? Do we expect God to answer the prayer we prayed this morning by night or at the latest by tomorrow? You might have prayed for the same person for years and you see no change, so you say, "If God hasn't answered in this length of time, will He ever answer?" "Should I give up?" Jesus' answer to all requests is clear, "Keep on asking, Keep on seeking, Keep on knocking."

We know of a miracle that has occurred recently. A person had cancer and it had gone to the liver and there seemed to be no hope. The treatments were terrible, but with many prayers the last report was, "cancer free". This is just one example of answered prayers of Christian people. God always answers our prayer, but we are to pray for His Will to be done. Sometimes He answers no, sometimes it is later, and sometimes yes. As we pray we should be persistently seeking His will. God will always answer in the right time and in the right way. Make your requests known to Him, He is listening.

Read: Luke 11:9 & 10

*T*here are two sisters in the Bible that tell us a great deal about Jesus. We just need to look at the Scripture and think about the messages. The two sisters, Mary and Martha and their brother lived together and were good friends to Jesus. We find they thought their friend would always be there to help them. We see the sisters have very different personalities, but Jesus loved them both. This tells us that Jesus loves us even when we do not put Him first. We also see that Jesus weeps with us when we have sorrows. Evidently Mary thought His Word was the most important and Martha thought her job as hostess held priority. Also we see them thinking Jesus should have been there when their brother, Lazarus was ill, because they knew He could have healed him. They were not thinking of the perfect plan of Jesus when both said, "if you had been here, he would not have died." We see them thinking "what is the reason to obey Jesus by rolling the stone away, since he has been dead so long?"

Do we see the message of Jesus always being on time for a reason or reasons we do not see? Do we see Him telling Martha to do the most important? I also think we can see ourselves in these two sisters. Sometimes we have little faith and wonder why Jesus was not there. We, as Christians should remember He is always there and He has plans that will be carried out.

Read: John 11:21; 25, 26, 32, 39-43

We are in the Easter Season, and I have wondered many times why the day of Christ's death is called Good Friday when it was the day that Jesus was crucified. Looking for an answer, this one seemed to be the right one. Jesus came to save, came to sacrifice Himself for mankind, to take all our sins on Himself and shed His blood so that we could go directly to the Father. People had tried animal sacrifice and keeping the law of God and this was not a lasting thing. When a person accepts Jesus as Lord and Savior, it is forever.

When we observe Good Friday, we are really observing the goodness of God and why is it called good when Jesus did so much suffering? Because God's good and perfect plan is completed for all people. Now, all a person has to do is to come to Jesus, with a contrite, repentant heart, asking Him to forgive and save and it is done. Jesus has paid the price and is our High Priest, our mediator between us and God. Jesus went willingly to the cross and completed the job He was born to do. Read about His arrest.

Read: Matthew 26:53-56

*L*et us look at the Mount of Transfiguration this morning. Jesus was showing His disciples about the glorified body at this time. The glorified body will be the body we have when Jesus comes back and we go to meet Him. When we look in the Bible an see Jesus talking to those who had been dead many, many years, we realize a person's life never ends. We might leave this earth and our soul go to be with the Lord, if we belong to Him, and even though our body will be buried, etc. there will come a time when the soul and body will be reunited.

When we think of Moses, and remember he was not allowed to go into the promised land, we also see that no man knew where he was buried. We look at Elijah and see that He went up in a chariot of fire. God has given us these Scriptures so that we will understand we never die. Do you know why the body is buried in the traditional position? Because when the person sits up he or she will be facing the east.

Read: Matt: 24:27 and Matt. 17:1-3

*W*hat a great, great blessing when we observe the Easter Season! It isn't a day to put eating and having a party first, but a day to be thankful to the one that was willing to hang on a cross and shed His precious blood, so we could inherit eternal life. It could have ended with His death and burial, but we have the beautiful news of His resurrection.

We can know we will not die and stay in the grave, but arise to be with our Savior and Lord. When a person accepts Jesus, ask Him to come into heart, and determines to live for Him, he or she inherits eternal life. In other words we become joint heirs with Jesus Christ. He arose and ascended and went back to Heaven to prepare a place for us. Have a blessed Sunday Season, worshiping the Lord.

Read: Matthew 28:1-6

My Prayer this morning: " Dear Lord, help me to be a blessing to someone today. I know someone needs encouraging, someone needs to know You hear their prayer, someone has terrible health problems, and someone does not know you and are in need of a good Christian friend to guide them." We celebrate the resurrection of our Lord. We know the suffering He faced because of His great love for each of us. We also know the happiness of His coming out of that grave and His teachings for the next forty days and His ascension.

If you are not familiar with all these happenings, please open your Bibles and you will read the most beautiful story ever told. Jesus did not have to shed His Blood for us, but He laid down His life willingly. When you become discouraged think on these things. You are loved! If you had been the only person in the world, Jesus would have suffered and died for you. He loves you that much! So, if you have trouble and are discouraged this morning, lift up your head, Jesus is present.

Read: Psalm 24:9 & 10 and Psalm 27:1

Many times we have the thought of "just giving up" and that is an idea Satan plants in peoples' minds. During the life of a Christian, there is no giving up, but just keep on serving Jesus each day. Did the disciples give up when they thought Jesus was gone? It seems that they did, because we find Peter telling the others he was going fishing and they went with him. They were going back to the place Jesus called from in the beginning. As long as Jesus was near there was no problem of giving up or going back to their old job, but when they could not see Him, this was the first thing they wanted to do.

Are we the same? When we feel Jesus close, we are happy, thankful and prayerful, but what about the times when we feel that He is not hearing us, that He is far away? When I was a child, I was taught when a job seemed hard to grit my teeth and do it anyway. That is the way a Christian needs to think at all times. Jesus has not left you, but you have gotten away from Him, so in those times let us "grit our teeth" and pray for guidance and do the job, anyway. Let us ask Jesus to clear the way and show us what He wants us to do for His Glory. Jesus is near, call on Him for strength!

Read: John 21:1-6

Why do we worry and fret over things? Oh yes, we Christians are guilty of this very thing. When we worry and fret we are really saying, "I don't believe God's Word and I don't trust Him." Do you remember the song that says "His Eye Is On The Sparrow?" We need to depend on Father God.

A father protects and provides for his children, as long as they are with him. We tell everyone we are a child of God, so why all the anxiety? Where is our faith? Anxiety will creep in and that is the time for us to surrender it all to our Father. He has not left us and we do not need to allow Satan to put the "what if" thoughts into our minds. We can think of a dozen bad things that might happen and that is a "what if." Are you having a day of worry and fret? Just begin depending on your heavenly Father, He is near, call on Him today.

Read: Luke 12:23-28

I was reading a story of a child who was lost from his mother for a short time. He searched and searched and could find her nowhere. He thought she had abandoned him and he began crying and was very afraid. This is just like a Christian when they feel God is not hearing their prayer, feel that He has abandoned them in troubled times. We have to remember we are the ones who have moved away from God. He is in the same place He has always been. We have allowed Satan to get to us and cause us to doubt or cause us to hold a grudge or something else. When we do not feel the presence of God in our lives, what should we do?

The Bible tells us to draw near to God and He will draw near to us. This can be done by prayer and reading God's Word. Should we go searching for Him as the little boy did? When the child found his mother she told him, "you are my son, I will never leave you." That is the promise we are given, but we are to watch our conversation or our lives.

Read: Hebrews 13:5 & 6 and Psalm 46:1

*L*et us think of the "blame game" this morning. When you have a loved one that you know is on the wrong track, away from the Lord, will not listen to you when you try to talk to him or her, do you blame yourself for not saying enough in the past, not showing enough care, not taking enough time to talk to the person? We stay awake at night thinking, "If only I had done this or that". We pray, and see no change and ask, "doesn't God want everyone to be saved, everyone to serve Him?" Yes, God is pursuing your loved one, His love is boundless, He died to save sinners and His grace does not stop. You ask, "what am I to do?"

The answer is this: Keep on praying, live as you know God would have you live, and trust that your loved one is being chased by God. He will give that person chance after chance to turn to Him, but we know that salvation is up to the individual, because God did not create robots. I have known of a person praying for a child and after the person dies, the prayers are answered. The child became a devout Christian.

Don't give up, trust in God!

Read: Rev. 5:8 and Psalm 55:22

*H*ow many times have you heard someone pray and the prayer was so beautiful, you wished you could pray like that? I have heard so many people say they could not pray a pretty prayer. God does not listen to a prayer because it is pretty, but when it is from the heart. This is a beautiful gift given to us by Jesus. When He died on the cross the veil of the temple was rant or torn from top to bottom. The hand of God was the one that tore this thick veil and He was showing everyone they did not need to go to a high priest to get their prayers answered, but could pray directly to God.

Jesus is now our mediator (go between) as we pray. What a wonderful thing He did for us making it possible to pray at any time and also knowing He shed His precious blood to save us once for all. Before this the people had to stand without the temple and wait to see if their sins were forgiven.

Remember, we are to forgive others and just talk to Jesus, He will hear you any hour of the day!

Read: Colossians 3:13 and Colossians 4:2

Do you seek the counsel of Jesus Christ before you make a decision? If you do not, how do you think your life would be different if you stop making "snap" decisions and ask the one perfect counselor to show you the right decision. He is available night or day and we have the assurance of knowing we are not alone. Isaiah 28:29 tells the Lord gives wonderful advice.

We will find wisdom and guidance when we prayerfully seek and trust God for our answers. His wisdom is vast and knows no bounds. In other words I think of this, God knows all, sees all, directs all according to His will. He knows the future and we grumble about things many times when God has only acted for our good. Before Jesus ascended He promised He would send another comforter, which is the Holy Spirit. Jesus supplied us with all we need. Just call on Him and ask for wisdom.

Read: John 14:16 and John 14:2

The Bible tells us to set our affection on things above and not on earthly things. How do we show others the importance of letting Jesus take the reins of our lives? If someone makes a mistake and you are sure they could have done better, how do you react to them? You could ruin their day by what you say, by the harshness with which you react or you could make their day with loving kindness and patience.

We have a choice, as Christians , to live so that others will see the love of Jesus in us, or think we are horrible people and dislike us. Let us remember when we set our affection on Jesus, when we put loving Him and living for Him first, thanking Him and becoming more like Him in our dealings with others, we will show Jesus to those around us. My prayer today: Lord, thank You for being near when I feel crushed and overwhelmed and help me to always show kindness to others.

Read: Luke 9:23

We saw so much on TV yesterday, and I pray that all our friends are OK. When we see destruction all around we realize material things are not the main things, and when lives are spared we just want to forget the material things and thank God. The most important thing for each individual is to be ready to meet God. Of course we want to live as long as we can with our loved ones, but we all know that one day our physical lives will end.

We do not know the day or the hour, which is good, but we have an opportunity to get ready to live in such an awesome place where no storms or troubles will ever come again. We need to pray for victims of disasters and ask God to give them wisdom and help them with their losses and if they are not saved, to show each one the brevity of life. Talk to Jesus in your sorrow and troubles, and know He is there, He will hear!

Read: Psalm 50:15 & Psalm 120:1

*W*e might think of our souls as workshops. When Christ comes into our workshop, He wants room to work. He is the Master Craftsman and He will bring His tools with Him. Our responsibility is to clear the clutter so that He will have room to work. Do you have hate, sinful habits that you want to hold onto and greed? If so, we must ask to be forgiven of these things and put them our of our lives.

Christ will bring in love, after the housecleaning is done. Spiritual housecleaning is letting go of those world desires and asking Christ to Clean up our lives. Invite Jesus into your workshop and ask Him to help you clean it up, because He has plans for your life, and His plans are more beautiful than anyone can imagine, call on Him today!

Read: 1st John 2:15-17

May

We might have days when we feel God is far away. Everything we try to do seems to be the wrong thing and we are frustrated. When we are in the midst of one of those days, let us remember God is near. He has said, "I know the plans I have for you" (Jeremiah 29:11) God knows us before we are born and there is a job for each of us, but human nature, being what it is, we sometimes refuse to follow these plans for out lives. God gave each of us the ability to choose. Because He loves us, He has provided us a way to have a personal relationship with Him. He gave His Son, Jesus to die on the cross as a payment for our sin. Yes, even though we have accepted Jesus as Savior and Lord we have days that seem to be an absolute disaster to us.

When we arose, we had specific plans for the day, but many things happened to throw us off track and when we went to bed that night we felt like a failure. Was the entire day a waste? Have we considered the fact that a day like this might be how God chose to teach us to realize things will not always be the way we want them to be. Jesus was interrupted many times as the woman touched the hem of His garment, and the blind man begging by the road. What is our answer to days like the above? Ask God to help you to drop your expectations and ask Him for His plan because God always has something better for us. After Jesus had been tempted by the devil, we find angels ministering to Him, and He was ready to begin His public ministry. He heard of John, being cast into prison, but He did not go because John had fulfilled his ministry and Jesus knew God's plan for Him. Instead, He began to preach.

Read: Matt. 4:12-20

We look at the news and see the terrible state of our world today, and we ask, "what has happened to the 'old Paths' or the way things were before?" God created a perfect world, but Satan has done His best to prove the prize creation of God will turn from Him. We need only to look at the Book of Job to see the great deceiver trying to make a person belonging to God "curse God and die". Again, we look at a wonderful, awesome, loving God who forgives us and shows us the way we need to live. The world is in a state of rebellion, and our Nation cannot be called a Christian Nation anymore, because the majority has gotten away from God.

There are many who do not want guidance or any laws. We see corruption from the leaders of our country. Everyone is looking for popularity and profit. We see people who are told looting other people's property is O.K. There is no thought to the fellow man and how hard he or she has worked to build a place that will be burned. Lawlessness abounds, but we know Jesus is coming soon to set every thing in order. God has promised destruction to the wicked. Christians, we need to pray for God to work in our lives and Nation.

Read: Isaiah 5:20-24

As we look into God's Word we see the compassion of Jesus in the miracles He performed. Jesus, the Messiah fulfilled the prophecy in Isaiah. "The Spirit of the Lord God is upon Me, because the Lord has anointed Me to preach good tidings to the poor, He has sent me to heal the brokenhearted, to proclaim liberty to the captives, and the opening of the prison to those who are bound, to proclaim the acceptable year of the Lord." (Isaiah 61: 1 & 2) Jesus gave these old prophets messages hundreds of years before the events. The promises of God are always sure. We do not know the time or place they will happen, but be assured what God promised will come to pass in His time.

The Pharisees were loyal to a code of conduct that had been taught by Moses. Their minds were closed to the voice and actions of Jesus. Do Christians have dogmatic beliefs today, because they were taught by someone? If you find yourself in this state, think about what the Pharisees missed by not listening to Jesus Christ and believing in Him. We have His Word, which is clear, and we need to go to God's Word instead of trying to follow traditions. We go to the words of David, "Teach me Thy way, Oh Lord, and lead me in a plain path." We, as children of God, are not to become discouraged as we listen to the news, but pick up God's Word and lift up our heads.

Read: Psalm 24:3-5 & chapter 25:4 & 5

Do you have times when you feel that God is far away. Times when you know you have grown spiritually cold. This is because we each live in a world with many cares and burdens and we try to take care of those cares by working harder or some other way. This is not the way we are taught in God's Word. After a person accepts Jesus Christ, he or she becomes one of the family of God. With God as the Father who is available to listen to us all the time. But, as time goes on, we do not talk to the Father as much and we do not study the Word, which is God talking to us. Because of this neglect in communication, we do not feel that God is near or interested in our troubles. Of course, we are all wrong because God never leaves us. We are the guilty ones because we have wandered away from Him by our carelessness or we might say neglect. Because of the distance we have wandered, we have grown spiritually cold. We are not dead, spiritually, but we appear to be so and we know the only One who is able to renew us is Jesus. Before we are converted or we say saved we are as the young man, who was dead and brought to life, so we could say a cold corpse became a living, breathing person when Jesus arrived.(Luke 7: 13-15) Can't we see that Jesus cares so much He was willing to die that we might have an abundant and eternal life. What is our solution? Go to the One who died for you, ask Him to forgive all the neglect and draw you closer and once again let you feel His nearness.

Read: Psalm 51:12 & 15

How do we worship our God? Some people might pray to Him standing with heads bowed, and others might feel they should be on their knees. The position does not matter, but if our worship is not from the heart (innermost being) it is no good. God sees all and knows the thoughts we have so He knows if we are worshiping Him in truth and in spirit. We need to stop and think on the blessings of our Heavenly Father. There is no way we, as humans, can thank Him enough for all He has done for us. He has been our buckler and shield, a present help in time of trouble. We find that David had learned this and when he returned to God asking Him to restore the joy of God's salvation, he realized what God meant to him.

When a Christian gets away from God, he or she cannot be happy, because they know that there is much missing in their lives. Only when he or she returns to God will they know how to worship Him. Only then, will they realize what He means to them. David realized that God was his rock, his fortress (protection or keeper) who had delivered him. (Psalm 18: 1 & 2) Let us, each, search our hearts today and if we have gotten away from God, may we remember the Lord is the strength of my life. What am I without Him? As we go to Him in worship let us pray as David prayed.

Read: Psalm 9:1 and Psalm 19:14

*W*hen Jesus does a work in a person, is it hard for that person to explain all that happened? When a person is converted is it hard to explain that they were once blind, but now the eyes are opened and they can see? Do people understand the open eyes are the insight we have on spiritual things? There is no way to make a person understand these things until they accept Jesus. The blind man, who had been blind all his life and had sat and begged of others, was healed by Jesus. When his parents were asked about this they replied, "We know this is our son who was born blind, but who hath opened his eyes, we know not, ask him." When the people called Jesus a sinner, the man who had been blind answered them, "Whether he be a sinner or not one thing I know, whereas I was blind, I now can see."

Did you ever think of a person that would not accept Jesus, walking in darkness? They are blind to the truth of God's Word. The light came to the world and dwelt among men.

Read: John 9:1-5

We have choices in life. We can choose to have a positive attitude or we are free to choose to become negative about everything around us. When someone inquires about how you are doing, do you answer as one friend of mine, "I am blessed", or do you tell all about your pains and aches and cause the person to feel bad for you? If you see a person who is having a bad day, are you able to lift him or her up by making them see their blessings or have a laugh or two?

Each morning when we wake up we have two choices. We choose to be in a good mood or a bad mood. We can go through the day grumpy and ugly to those around us or we can choose to think of our blessings and show a happy face. Which do you think is the one a Christian should have to show their faith and joy in serving God? Life is all about choices, we can choose to live fully or we can choose to be negative and sad.

Read: Jeremiah 17:7 & 8

May 8

*W*hat does the word service mean to you? Does it mean going to church on Sunday and maybe on Wednesday Night? Are we willing to sacrifice some of our time in the Name of the Lord, to those who need us? Jesus showed us the real meaning of service when He washed the feet of the disciples' feet. This was a servant's job. When people came into the house with dusty feet, the servant was the one to wash their feet and this was done, we might say, in the master's name. The servant worked for the master and did his bidding. The disciples, knowing that Jesus was the Messiah would not have been able to understand this gesture except it be a lesson taught by Jesus.

Are we willing to devote more time to the Master? Are we willing to do jobs for Him that are hard and thankless? Have I encouraged someone this week? Have I helped someone in need this week? Have I taken time to pray for those in trouble this week? Jesus would say, "do you love Me"?

Read: John 13:12-116

*F*rom some of Corrie Ten Boon's books comes this message: "There is not a pit that is so deep that God is not deeper still". Sometimes in this life we feel despair and feel as though we are in a deep pit. We feel that our cries go unheard and finally we just whimper and pray. Where is God,when this happens?" He is right there in the pit with you and knows the troubles that sent you into that pit.

You could have had abandonment, grief, fear, and depression. God wants to bring you up out of the pit, to raise you up to sunshine and fresh air, to enliven you so that you will be able to serve again. What is the answer? As Corrie Ten Boon did in all her captivity and awful trials, Grab onto God and don't let go. He is there, call on him until He answers you!

Read: Psalm 40:1-3

$\mathcal{R}$ecently, I enjoyed preparing a Sunday School Lesson from the Book of Genesis that I want to share: Actually John 1:1 is right for the first verse because Jesus was with God from the beginning. We know that Genesis is a Book of beginnings, and we also know that anything God creates is perfect, so from my study I see that something happened between the first and second verse. It makes sense to me that this would be the time Satan was cast out of heaven and some of his angels with him. (Jude 1:6) There was an upheaval on earth because of God's divine judgment.

It is written in Jeremiah again that the earth was void and it had no light. When the Spirit of God moved there was light and darkness had to flee. We should remember Satan was once an angel in Heaven, but pride and jealously are the sins I see as the reason he was cast out. We see that God made of the earth a new beginning. Study your Bible and you will find it more interesting than you can imagine. Jesus tells the seventy He saw Satan when he was cast out.

Read: Luke 10:17 & 18

May is the month we honors our Mothers. There are some today who do not want to become parents, but it is the greatest opportunity you will have in this life coupled with serving Jesus Christ. As a parent you have the opportunity to teach your child about Jesus. The teaching process is not just telling but showing your child or children they are to walk in faith. The fact is this: you might tell me for many hours, but if I see you doing the things you have told me not to do, your talking will mean nothing to me.

Do you ever talk and talk and think your child is not listening? Do you think you will tell him or her today and they will forget the lesson tomorrow? Do you remember the things you were taught as you were growing up? Do you remember your home life during those years? Of course, and your children will remember the things you tell them in later years. The "growing up" years are most important because even though they might not think so, it is the time of learning that will mold their lives. I remember my mother praying for me, and teaching me to use the language a lady should use, and many other rules, sometimes with a switch if I did not obey. Yes, I remember a Christian Mother that I thought too strict, but I remember with love.

Read: 2nd Timothy 1:3, 12 & 13

*H*ome. When we think of home we think of a place we can rest, a place we have made comfortable, a place with our loved ones. When we get home we are able to put our feet up and relax. Home is where everyone knows your weaknesses and love you anyway. I am talking about the home we have on earth, but there is a heavenly home for the Christian. This will be a perfect place with rest for those who are weary, those who have had pain and much suffering on earth will be in a place of no pain.

There will be no need for light in this beautiful place, because God is the light. While we are on earth we have pitfalls, and unpleasant surprises, but not so in our heavenly home. Everyone will know and love you and there will be no envy or jealously there. Let us enjoy our earthly home, but look forward to the life eternal in this beautiful heavenly home.

Read: Rev. 21:4 & 22:5

𝒟o you remember your mother's retort when you said, "everybody else is doing it" or" everybody else gets to go there". Most of the time the mother would say, "if everybody else jumped off a cliff, would you want to jump too". We need to set our standards high and refuse to look at others' actions that are against God's Word. We, as Christians should remember we are only responsible for ourselves. The Bible is the guideline and yes the lifeline for us. In our society to go against the flow might be uncomfortable many times because when no one stands with you, it is hard to stand up for the things you know are right before God.

Let us remember that we are never alone, even though it feels that way numerous times. Jesus is standing right beside you giving you the strength to do the right thing and you never know the influence you have on others who are watching you. Be an inspiration to those around you!

Read: Matt. 7:13-14

*D*id you ever watch running water? Of course and we notice the water always goes to the lowest point. There is a lesson in this for us. Jesus washed the disciples feet showing Himself a servant and He always gave everything to the Father, never taking honor for Himself. In fact He poured Himself out and went to the lowest point for each of us. We want people to love us, to show us consideration, and to treat us kindly because we are generous and we think it only fair to be treated well by everyone else.

When we feel this way, are we putting ourselves first? Do we do good deeds to be recognized by others? Do we serve the Lord to be recognized by those around us? What does all this mean? It means self-denial and that is putting the interest of others before our own. When we show our love by pouring ourselves out, we get down to the way we should show our love for Christ and for others. This is the last testimony of John the Baptist.

Read: John 3:27-30

You hear this: "I just cannot believe the Bible", but when you ask about an incident in History the same person will tell you they know it happened. Faith is believing without seeing. Do we have faith in some things and then refuse to believe the most important Word of God? We might think of calming the sea and say, "can't be done", but it was done by Jesus.

The virgin birth, you might say impossible, but with God all things are possible, and Jesus, His Son, came from Heaven as a baby, born of a virgin and grew up to teach and be crucified so that we might have eternal life. There are those who say, "I cannot be a Christian, because I don't believe these things". Are you willing to believe the History of two thousand years ago or do you stop at believing the history of a few hundred years ago? You might never understand why this or that event happened to you, but God is pleased when you have the faith to know He is in control of it all. There are a number of reasons things could happen for good, that we cannot see. Did this happen to make me depend on God more? Did this happen to make me a stronger Christian? Is that person in heaven where there will be no more pain? God knows the answers.

Read: John 20:29

We wake up to a beautiful day and think we do not have a worry in the world. We pray a little, thanking God for allowing us to awake to a new day and then we are blindsided by something that will knock us down. This is the work of Satan. He does not want to see a happy Christian, enjoying life and if he can bring on trouble, he will. You think, "I cannot handle this" and maybe you go back to bed wanting to pull the covers over your head and suddenly you think, "what am I doing here?" "I know God is with me, because He promised never to leave me alone." and you know it is time to talk to Him, to petition Him, asking for strength and help to solve the problem and if that is impossible, asking Him for the strength to get you through the situation.

I pick up my Bible and begin praying for God to show me what I need, and I start reading His Word. There is the message that will help me because Jesus said He would go away so the Comforter could come and live with me, advise me, comfort me. Satan is defeated! I have turned to God in all my troubles and He heard me!

Read: James 4:7 and Hebrews 4:16

When you pray, do you remember your Pastor and his wife? They get many requests from the members of the church and others, but they need prayer, also. There are many burdens other people do not know, because a pastor and his wife cannot confide to others as we, their flock, can. Most people would say, "they are close to God, and need nothing, their life is easy". The easy part is not true, but if you ask them they would not trade their work for God with anyone else. You see, when God calls you into a work, He is there with you.

No matter how many hardships you have there is joy in serving the Lord! How do I know this? I have been a Pastor's wife and when we were working so hard in our church, I enjoyed knowing we were in the will of the Heavenly Father. Even though everyone is not pastors or pastors' wives, when we are serving God we will be happy. Does this mean people will not have troubles? No, but remember the poem "Foot Prints" and know that Jesus is always with you.

Read: Psalm 23

*D*o we really care about those around us? Sometimes we care and want to help, but then we think of the sacrifice as being too great. I would fix a meal for the person who is ill, but I am so busy and the distance is too great, I'll do it another time. I would volunteer but our schedule is filled to capacity, or we would give our tithe today, but our finances are too tight. These are some of the excuses we might use to keep us in our comfort and yes, our selfish zone.

When we really care we do not focus on ourselves and the sacrifices we make. The sacrifice becomes a part of the activity and the rest is wrapped up in the love for God, love for others and the desire to serve. The Holy Spirit is asking you to really care and happy you and I will be when we willingly obey Him. Our lives will overflow with joy and love.

Read: Romans 12:1

$\mathcal{D}$o we want to live a holy life? Someone might say," Oh, no, I have seen those people who think they are better than others" or I have seen a person who is a holier than thou person", and I don't want to have that kind of life. This kind of life is not the holy life for Christ. The true holy life for Christ does not mean a person is perfect (no person has ever been perfect except Jesus Christ). Holiness is not something to slap others with or to make yourself feel better.

A true Christian will never think of himself or herself better than another person. Instead a holy life is one of generous service to God and others. The person realizes that God looks on each person the same and each person is responsible to Him. A holy life is one that will serve the Lord humbly, with gladness and thankfulness. What does God have for you to do?

Read: Micah 6:8

*D*id you know that many times we suffer disappointments because God is getting us set up for His appointments? We see that Mary and Martha had to be very disappointed when Jesus did not come to their brother, Lazarus, when he was very ill. The man that went to Jesus because his little girl was dying would have been disappointed when he saw Jesus take time to heal the woman with the issue of blood. The greatest disappointment for the disciples would be seeing Jesus hang on a cross and die. They had thought He would set up His kingdom on earth. They had loved and followed Him, heard Him teach lessons that burned into their hearts, saw Him as He healed, cast out demons and cleansed the temple. They are disappointed to see Him die, because they did not expect Him to end this way. BUT we see the appointments Jesus was keeping during these times.

He raised Lazarus from the dead, brought life into the little girl after healing the woman with the issue of blood and died on the cross, shedding His blood so that we each can be saved, and after His appointment with death HE AROSE AGAIN, and ascended into Heaven to sit on the right hand of the Father, God, and prepare a place for us.

Read: Acts 2:7-9

*T*here are times we find ourselves feeling as though God has turned away from us because we pray and pray and nothing happens. Let us take note of ourselves. How much have I studied His Word, lately? Am I the one who has gotten away from His Teachings? When good things were happening did I forget to thank Him ? You see, God has not left you, He has been there all the tine. We human beings have a tendency to get away from Him, because of the everyday temptations we face. He has told us "I will never leave you or forsake you". So, why does He not answer my prayer?

God always answers prayer, but His answer is not always yes. His answer could be "wait" or it could be "no, my child, this is not what you need." It could be "this is something you must bear to make you a stronger Christian". I think of Paul when he prayed three times for God to remove the thorn in his flesh, and God told him, "no, My grace is sufficient". We should remember God is with us through all our life and when our work is finished on this earth, He will take us home. The Father was there when the son returned to Him.

Read: Luke 15:18-20

Commitment in God's Work is a word we hear little about these days. Why? People have to sign notes, mortgages, and many other promises to pay off loans, but when there is work to be done in the churches, they hesitate to take positions. Some will say I do not have time and others will say they are not capable of doing the task, and yet others will take on a task and do it for a few weeks and then leave it for someone else. If we promise to take on a job to do for the Glory of God, which is the reason any job in the church should be done, let us be conscious of finishing it. If you promise to do a job and the cost and demands are greater than you thought they would be, remember if you are a woman or man of faith and depending on the Lord to help you. He will.

How hard the job must have been for Jesus. He had critics, persecutions, the temptations of Satan and many who would not believe His teachings, yet, He finished His course. Let us, each, pray for guidance in everything we do for God, asking Him to be with us, giving us strength to finish the course He has for us.

Read: Matthew 18:11-14.

$\mathcal{D}$o we try to reason things out and remind God that we know what we should do and the results we should have when we do His work? We find a character in God's Word who thought he should tell God about Saul and the persecution he had brought to the saints. We might say, "how did Ananias forget that God knew all about Saul?" When God called him, Ananias seemed willing to answer and do His bidding, but when he heard the task, he was ready to argue with God.

When God calls you and me, do we think we have all the answers and need to tell God who will listen and who will not. Are we quick to say, "oh, I have talked to that person before and he or she belongs to a group who do not believe, so there is no need of going back to the same person?" Do we underestimate the power of God on other people's lives? God did not take the excuse from Ananias but said, "Go". Of course we see God had already done His work on Saul and had him prepared to hear His Word. The important lesson, here, is to obey the leadership of God without question.

Read: Acts 9:10-15

Did you ever hear someone compare leprosy to sin? Leprosy was such a dreaded disease in the Bible and there was no cure for it. We see very little of this today, but going back to the comparison let us think of it. This disease was a slowly progressing thing. It could begin in a finger or a toe and spread to the body slowly eating away the joints until the person died. When a person goes against God's Word, he or she does not jump into wrong-doing all at once. A young healthy person is tempted to use just a little addictive substance at first hearing, "it won't hurt you." But when they listen to this temptation, there will be other times and the drug or alcohol grows on them and many people find themselves in the "gutter" because they have gradually gotten into something that will destroy the body.

Just like leprosy, when a person becomes a drug addict or alcoholic, the cure is Jesus Christ. First, let us stay away from those things that will be so harmful to the body and mind. If we have been involved and have a craving for these things, go to Jesus and ask Him to help you, giving you strength to take care of the body He has given you. We find He was the only cure for leprosy.

Read: Mark 1:40-42

Remembering Memorial Day, celebrated in May, we need to thank God for our freedom. There are many in this world who would give anything to have the freedom to worship as we do. When I hear someone say, "I do not salute the flag" I feel very sorry for that person, because they do not realize that we live in the greatest country on earth because of the sacrifice of many men and women as they fought to keep our freedom. Also, think about the mothers and dads who lost their children for this freedom. We take the blessings of God so lightly and people who are corrupt will stand and say , "God bless America". Can they mean this, when they are only thinking about themselves and the power they want and this is just a statement to appease people.

My prayer today is, "Thank you God for each person who fought for this freedom we have, and we know you were with our country because of the praying people, Help us to become a Christian nation again, putting you first." "And Dear Heavenly Father, wake our leaders up and show them the need for all of us to serve you". God is waiting for us to show Him we love Him.

Read: Psalm 50:23 and 46:1-3

We must remember our young men and women who have fought through the years to keep America safe. I want to say a sincere "Thank you" for each sacrifice that has been made for our country. We need, also, to remember to thank God for keeping us safe. I am sure without Him we would not have survived the battles we have seen. People tend to say, "I did it", Yes, you did your part, but without God's help we would all be miserable failures.

We are not the country we could be and we are not the country we were at one time, but let us pray for God to lift us up and help us become the country He would be pleased with. When we ask God to bless America, let us mean it! God hears our prayers and the prayers of those who belong to Him are as a sweet savor in His nostrils. He is available for each person and our country.

Read: Hebrews 13:5 & 6

"In the beginning was the Word and the Word was God and the Word was with God" This is one of my favorite verses, because it tells me Jesus was with God during all His creative Work. After Jesus had fed the five thousand plus people with the loaves and fishes they were following Him. Were they thinking He would furnish them their next meal?

Jesus knows the heart of each person, the thoughts, the reasons for doing things. He knew these people were seeking after what they could get from Him and they also wanted signs from Him. Yes, Jesus gives us our needs on this earth, but these earthly things perish and the lesson He was teaching the people was they could labor for food, and it would perish, but the important thing was not these perishable things, but the food that would last forever.

Only Jesus can supply the Bread of Life. The people asked Jesus, "What sign will you give us, because we remember the history of our fathers eating manna in the desert"? Then He told them He was the Bread of Life who had come down from Heaven to save the lost.

Read: John 6:34-38

1 think, many times, of the little old lady we saw in the Holy Land. We were in the cave that was supposed to be the place of Jesus' Birth when she came in dressed all in black. She entered blowing kisses and placed her coins in a container and bowed blowing kisses as she backed out. She was honoring God. We give of our abundance and many times do not stop to thank God that we have finances to tithe. We have the story of Jesus watching the poor widow as she gave her two mites. This was all she had, and she would have to trust God for her next meal.

The lesson, here, is not the amount she gave, which would have amounted to a little change in our day, but from the heart she was worshiping the Lord. Her gift showed that she was giving herself entirely to God and trusting Him for her future. The way she used her money disclosed here moral and spiritual condition. The first commandment is "Thy shall love the Lord with all thy heart, soul, and mind." Let each of us take inventory this morning. Do I love the Lord this much? Do I trust Him with everything?

Read: Mark 12:41-44 and Mark 12:30

We might hear a person say this: "I have been such and such in my life and God cannot use me" or I have nothing to give and God cannot use me". We will look in the Bible and see how God chose to use different people and yes, He wants to use you. He used Abraham and Sarah, an immigrant couple, to have a child in their old age to found the Israelite nation. He used Joseph, hated by his brothers and sold into slavery, to save his family from starving during a famine. He chose Moses, a baby marked for slaughter, to lead His people out of Egypt. These are just a few from the Old Testament and later we see God using a young virgin to be the mother of Jesus and Saul, a persecutor of Christians, being converted to become one of the greatest missionaries in the Bible.

There are many more characters throughout the Scriptures that God used in a great way and looking at all these. we know He can use anyone. God can and will use us in each walk of life if we are willing to follow Him. Jesus has promised to help us.

Read: John 14:16-18

*W*e, as Christians are to beware of greed. One of out great temptations is the temptation of covetousness. This begins with very small children in school when they look at the clothes other children have and want the same. Parents help this to grow when they go out and do their best to find the same name brands. As people grow older they begin coveting a car that someone else has, and later in life they will try to keep up with their neighbors, even when it gets them into financial trouble. Jesus warns about coveting. He knew the human being would be tempted to long for something he or she did not have and how they would look at others and long for what they have.

We are living in a society that is based on the foolish belief that the worth of a person is the amount of worldly possessions he or she owns. We must remember the warning that Jesus gave. We can covet money, status, power, beauty, intelligence and even spiritual blessings. This is one of Satan's greatest tools, but if we stop and think about the end of our lives, we should ask ourselves, "When I die what will I take with me"? We will realize the answer is "nothing, but what I have done for God."

Read: Luke 12:13-15 and then verses 16-21

Words come much easier than actions. When we look at the disciples and think of what they would say in talking about Jesus, we would think they would always be there for Him. Many times we speak before we think, make promises we do not keep. This is a blight on a Christian's life. If you say you will do something, do it, or be brave enough to face the person and explain why you cannot do it. Jesus asked the three to watch for Him while He prayed and in my imagination they would have said, "we will", but they slept. Peter, who had vowed to be loyal to Him, denied that he ever knew Him.

During the time of Jesus trial and hanging on the cross, His disciples fell apart. They scattered because of fear. BUT, Jesus is forgiving and these same disciples were the very ones who carried the gospel. We. as human beings, might fall apart sometimes, but Jesus will reach down and pick us up if we just turn to Him. He will forgive and use each of us for His Glory. After his denial, we find Peter becoming a great leader.

Read: Matthew 26:31-35

June

One thing God makes very clear in His Word is His love for us. We long to be loved by others in spite of our faults. Our friends know us by appearance. They smile when they see us but God knows us we would say "inside and outside" he knows our weaknesses and our strengths and He loves each individual. Isn't it wonderful to know He knows and loves every single person on the planet? Yes, He knows you. He knows your joys and fears. Are we willing to carry everything to Him in prayer?

Let us remember we are greatly loved by God who knows every single facet of our lives. We cannot imagine the forgiveness of God. Not one of us would be willing to give our child's life for people who are unthankful and hate us. This is the Lord's day, The day He arose after all the suffering He did for you and me. Let us rejoice, be thankful and be glad we have the privilege of going to worship Him.

Read: Psalm 139:1-6

We see a person, Simeon, in the Scriptures that we hear very little about. Evidently he was not an ordained religious leader and even though he had no credentials, he was a just and devout man, who had a close walk with God. His name means "God Hears" and he has patiently waited because it had been revealed to him by the Holy Spirit that he would see the Christ Child, before he died. We see a man of faith, patiently waiting for the one he knew was coming to save mankind. We do not know how long Simeon had been in the temple waiting, but we see a patient man. Do we have the patience and faith to wait on God to show us His Will for our lives?

God honors those who engage in quiet prayer and a lifetime of constant watchfulness for the Lord to come again. Somehow it had been revealed to Simeon that the Messiah would come as a baby, not as a great warrior. He also knew Christ's kingdom would be a stumbling block to some and the rock of salvation to others. As he blessed the Babe, Simeon also told Mary that a sword would pierce through her soul.

Read: Luke 2:15-30

*W*e think many things are "old fashioned " today. In the past a mother would teach her daughter to stay pure at all cost. She would be taught about God's Word and how to live after she was married. today, the only time we hear about something being pure it is the water we drink. "Drink pure bottled water" etc. The idea of purity in young men and women has been totally ignored and a beautiful part of God's creation has been scorned and forgotten. In everything we do, we need to remember God's way is the best way. In fact, it is the only way to live and be happy.

We need to look into His Word and follow His instructions and THAT IS NOT OLD FASHIONED, but will help us have clean lives because the Word shows us how to live.

Read: Psalm 119:1, 2 and 11

*H*ave you thought of the key test showing our commitment to Christ? It is our love for other believers. We express that love, not by words only, but by actions and attitudes. Jesus did not say that others would know us by our denomination, dress, or what we know, but by the way we love others.

During the last supper one of the followers, Judas, was so concerned with his greed that he was only thinking about where his gain would come from. Even earlier when the woman put the expensive ointment on the feet of Jesus, Judas had made the statement that it should have been sold and given to the poor. His mind was not on the poor but on getting that money into the bag he carried. Jesus knew his heart and knew he would betray him for silver. Judas' love for money was greater than his love for Jesus and we find many people who love money or wealth more than they love the Savior or others. Jesus knew exactly what Judas was going to do, because we find Him telling the remaining disciples, after Judas had gone out, that He would now be glorified. In other words He knew He would be pointed out by Judas soon.

Read: John 13:34

Should we question God? Absolutely not, but we are humans and when certain situations arise we want to ask God Why. We find people in the Scriptures questioning many times and this shows us they were human also. When we question, we are doubting His Word because He knows the plans He has for us and these are for our good. When God called Moses to go to the Pharaoh he questioned by saying he could not speak well. Also we find the people questioning why he was gone into the mountain so long and making a golden image to worship.

People want to do their own thing, many times, leaving God's Will out of their lives and that is one of the reasons for questioning...In other words it is as though they are saying, "But God don't I know best"? When God told Ananias to go to Saul, he questioned because he knew the persecution Paul had been responsible for. But, we have the story of obedience and how God used Saul, who later became Paul, to further the Gospel. Even though things were bad for the Children of Israel, God told them He knew the thoughts or plans He had for them, for their good.

Read: Jeremiah 29:11 & 12

*O*ne of my favorite characters In the Bible is Barnabas. Do you have a desire to encourage people? When a person makes the decision to live for Christ they need those who would help them grow by teaching and encouragement. We find Saul, who had been a persecutor of Christians until his encounter with Christ on the Damascus Road. People were afraid of him and Barnabas helped to move him to a place of ministry. We find him helping Saul, now Paul, to stabilize new believers at Antioch. When he launched out with Paul, it was Barnabas & Paul, but it became Paul and his party. Barnabas did not seek recognition but took the lead in defending Gentile believers before the Jerusalem Church. He later stood up to Paul about John Mark. He went with John Mark, encouraging a young man who later wrote a Book of the Bible.

We do not need to be recognized or popular to serve God. We can encourage and mentor, a person or persons that are in need and help them to grow and serve Him. Has God laid someone on your heart, someone that is hurting, someone who needs encouragement?

Read: Acts 9:26 & 27

God is not pleased with us when we "give up" and Satan knows this fact so he uses discouragement as one of his favorite tools to hinder Christians. When we look at Elijah, a great man of God, and see how he was so discouraged because of Jezebel and her threat we want to say, "after God has used and blessed you so much, why would you give up now, Elijah"? We find him becoming so depressed he has gone away into the wilderness. He even asked God to let him die, but he was told by the angel to get up and eat. Then, we find him going into a cave to live and God came to him asking him, "what are you doing here"? We find God speaking to him in a still voice and telling him that He is not alone, as he supposed, but there are seven thousand in Israel who still believed in God.

God wants us to trust Him, and we have been blessed numerous times, so we should never let satan use his tool of discouragement to make us want to "give up". God has the entire world in His Hands and he is certainly able to change things in our lives, He wants us to walk with Him and commune with Him, live in His will each day.

Read: Proverbs 3:5 & 6

We are quick to say "oh, that's just a little thing and it doesn't matter", but little things do matter. Too often we just want to focus on the big things and forget the small things in our lives. If we will be careful of the little things, we will then become strong enough to weather the big bumps or face the big things and ask God to help us through them. We can find ourselves using excuses, "I need a break" " I'm not hurting anyone" or "no one will know". These excuses will eat away at our character, undermining the strength we need to handle powerful temptations, making us weak Christians.

When we can't handle the small things in our lives, it follows we cannot handle the big things, either. We must willingly turn away from temptation to do wrong, even when we think no one else knows. God knows and sees all, even the little things.

Read: Ecclesiastes 12:13 & 14

We will think about anchors today. I heard a song yesterday, "My anchor holds" and even though I have heard it many times, I think the message is one we need to remember. Are you anchored in Jesus? When we go out on water in a boat we must have an anchor or we would keep floating when we wish to stop at a great fishing spot. The anchor will keep us steady and the boat will not be tossed about and so it is with us when we are not anchored in Jesus, we are not to be tossed about with every wind of doctrine. Our faith is to be anchored in the One who died so that we could have eternal life and He is sure and always there.

When we get away from Jesus and feel that He is not hearing our prayer, He has gone nowhere, He is waiting for us to come back and ask Him to forgive us our carelessness. In this life things change all the time and we do not know what tomorrow may bring, but we can be sure of one thing and that is the love of Jesus Christ and if we know Him, He will be with us to the end of this life and take us to Heaven to be with Him forever.

Read: Psalm 18:1-3

Do you desire a closer walk with Jesus? We. as Christians, are to be people who never give us. Is this going to cost you and me? Yes, sometimes our convictions for Jesus mght cost us a friend, or cause others to make remarks about us being "old fashioned" etc., but this does not matter to the person who is determined to live for Jesus at all cost. In order for us to have this closer walk we might have to give up some old habits or lose some sleep early in the morning in order to have quiet time with Hm.

The Pilgrim in Pilgrim's Progress had to go through all manner of sloughs and valleys on the way to the celestial city. But we know Jesus will walk with us through all the hardships we have. Walking with Him is priceless. Remember the poem footprints; when we can no longer walk, He will carry us if we follow Him. Life has many sloughs (hard times) and valleys (troubles), but give it to Jesus.

Read: Matthew 16:24-28

*F*orgiveness is the lesson Jesus taught on many occasions. Do you have trouble forgiving someone who has wronged you? Jesus showed that we could forgive even though we were beaten, spit upon, lied about and treated in horrible ways. When the paralytic was brought to Him, Jesus made the greatest statement of all when He said to the young man, "Thy sins are forgiven thee". We do not need to look back on our lives and say, "well, I haven't done what this person has, or I have lived a moral life before so Jesus had less to forgive". This is not true, because we are all sinners saved by grace when we accept Jesus Christ as our Savior and Lord. We do not need to look at other people and try to compare our lives with theirs. We will each stand before God and give an account of our life.

The power of forgiveness cannot be measured. Jesus challenged us, as His followers to forgive others who have wronged or hurt us. You might say, "I can't do that because this person or that did some bad things to me". I am sure they did not treat you as Jesus was treated and with His help we can forgive and we will be forgiven and happier people.

Read Mark 11:25 & 26

Does our society have a double standard for behavior? When the men dragged the woman caught in adultery to Jesus. she must have been utterly humiliated and disgraced. But, where was the man? Did he not commit the same sin as the woman? A double standard had crept into their society and so it is today. We look at a person with a lot of wealth. popularity and political power and excuse the actions we know are wrong, but when a person comes along with no money or prestige, he or she is scorned and judged to be less than a decent person. When Jesus said, "let him without sin, cast the first stone" or we might say judge, He is saying if you are not perfect yourself, you have no right to judge. He is the only perfect One and He will be the Judge.

When we look at this case in the Scriptures we find Jesus as the only one to decide the case and He told the woman to go and sin no more. Let us not be eager to point out the speck in another person's eye and ignore the plank in our own eye. If we have experienced forgiveness in our lives, we should desire to live in His grace, forgiving others and as Jesus commanded we should try "to sin more". Jesus knows we cannot live a perfect life, but we should try.

Read: John 8:3-7

When Jesus was on this earth there were many who refused to believe He was the Messiah, and so it is today. Even though we have the history of His life and the Sacrifice He made so we could be saved, there are numerous people who reject Him. Many others have called themselves Gods through the years and they are all dead, but people still follow the ideas they left.

For instance, in recent history we see Adolf Hitler who was a manipulater of many people. He thought he had the power to build a master race, but instead died by his own hand. We see kings in the Bible who claimed to be Gods, but Jesus is the only one who healed the sick, raised the dead and lived by the moral precepts He taught. He is the only one who conquered death. Many others have been called divine, but all have fallen short of God's Glory, except Jesus. Read this statement Jesus made and think on it.

Read: John 8:31 & 32

When we look at people what do we see that will make us form a good opinion? Is it wealth and beauty? Is it authority? Through the ages wealth has been the status used to tell if a person deserves respect. This should not be, but it is a human trait. There is much wealth which is not seen by the world. A person who has accepted Jesus as Savior and Lord is very wealthy, even though they are dressed in rags and have little to eat, and are homeless. You might ask, "how can this be, they have a miserable life"? They are very wealthy because Jesus went to prepare a place for them for eternity. This place will have streets of gold and more beauty than we can imagine. We think Fort Knox has all the gold to be desired, but that will be no comparison when we get to Heaven.

Let us not judge people by what they do or do not have, but love and encourage all we can because the Bible says we might entertain angels unaware. At the conclusion of your life, if you had only the clothes on your back, would you consider your life a success? We must remember this was the state of Jesus, who is seated at the right hand of the Father.

Read: Matthew 8:20

*D*o you believe God keeps all His promises? Absolutely! We are in the Book of Genesis in our Sunday School lessons and we see that God talked with Noah and instructed him and saved his family in the flood. God told him the rain would come even though it had never rained on the earth, before, and it came, just like He said. He promised Abraham and Sarah a child in their old age and the son was born just like He said.

Faith is believing what we cannot see. We are not to try to reason out the ways of God, because this is impossible, but by faith we must believe His promises, because they will come true. He has said He would come back for His own and He will come back in His time, JUST LIKE HE SAID. He has also promised to be with us to the end and this He will do.

Read: Acts 1:9-11

$\mathcal{N}$o matter who we are, what we do for a living, or how much wealth we have accumulated, we are bound to face struggles in life. It could be job loss, injury, illness, death of a loved one, or many other things to bring us down into a valley. When Job was in such terrible shape, one of his friends, Eliphaz, made this statement, " Man is born to trouble, as the sparks fly upward". (Job 5:7) There are those who blame God, those who blame other people, and sometimes even themselves when things are bad.

Sure, there is a place for human responsibility. The way we treat our bodies, the way we treat others, and getting into things we know are wrong by letting Satan lead us and forgetting God. It is our responsibility to live Godly lives and walk with the Lord, but those who do this, have troubles in their lives, also. Sometimes our troubles are to be used to glorify God as Jesus told the people who asked if the man was blind because of the sins of his parents.(John 9:1-3) But we must remember we fight spiritual wickedness in this world.

Read: Ephesians 6:10-13

$\mathcal{P}$eople seek after signs today, just as they did in Jesus' day. Jesus' answer to this was they were seeking after things other than God. They would look at the sky in the evening to tell the weather for tomorrow, but they wanted more. The unbelievers wanted Jesus to show them some great sign from heaven and then they would believe in Him. Today, people want to see something that is fantastic or a show of some kind instead of quietly worshiping from the heart. This is the reason for the handling of snakes, which the Bible never tells people to do. Paul accidently picked up the snake and it bit him and God took care of it, but we are not to tempt the Lord our God as the scribes and Pharisees were tempting Jesus.

Jesus told them to look at the only sign that was to be given and that was the sign of Jonah. He was in the belly of the whale three days and three nights and so Jesus was to stay in the grave three days and three nights and He would resurrect, Jonah was vomited out of the whale upon God's command. Jesus was saying you will know who I am when I arise.

Read: Matthew 16:1-4

*J*esus, the same yesterday, today and forever. He was with God in the beginning because we know He is the Word and "in the beginning was the Word and the Word was God and the Word was with God". The old prophets wrote that He was coming and He did, as God promised through them. He became flesh and dwelt among the people and was tempted by Satan as we are, resisting all the temptation Satan could throw at Him.

Now, the Son. Jesus, has spoken to us. He died so we might be saved, eternally, and then He sat down at the right hand of the Father God, sending the Holy Spirit to the earth to comfort all those who will believe in Him. He has give each of us a chance to become a fellow heir with Him and receive the same heritage. During the past, people looked forward to Jesus coming, but now, praise God, we can know He has come, fulfilled His mission and is our Mediator with the Father. WHAT A SAVIOR! We now have the promise He will come again to receive us to Himself.

Read: Hebrews 1:1-3

We have times in our lives when we feel discouragement and we feel that God is not going to answer our prayers. We have prayed for months about a situation and He remains silent. We see no result. I have heard of wives who prayed for years for an unsaved husband to have him finally come to Jesus. We are not to give up, but to realize our timing is not the same as God's timing. He has promised He will answer our prayers and that He will do, we do not know how, but He will answer in His time and in the best manner for us.

Even though we want to give up and stop praying for someone or something, a Christian should not even know the meaning of "giving up", because we have the promises of God and we know He always keeps His promises. God says by the Prophet Jeremiah, "I know the thoughts or plans I have for you"

Read: Jeremiah 29:11-13

*W*e all grow weary at times. It might be the job we are paid to do day by day and we know, as a Christian, we are to give a day's work for a day's pay. We see those around us "goofing" off and stealing time from the employer and we resent this because we are working hard at our job. So, we become weary and Satan would have us think, "what's the use, look at the things they get by with." Christians can become "burned out" doing good. Again, Satan would have them look around and see fellow Christian church members who have the attitude, "let someone else do it", and they become discouraged and weary and just want to quit. Paul addressed this when he wrote about the meals they had together in 2nd Thessalonians and reminded the people there they were to work if they were to eat.

Also Paul told the people not to be weary in well doing. What is our answer, then? We are to put our eyes on Jesus realizing we have a purpose for living and that purpose is to live for God and serve Him. We have a responsibility to influence others to work and pray knowing that God will never forget us, if we are His children.

Read: Isaiah 40:31

$\mathcal{A}$t some time in my life I have heard someone sing a song and the words have been in my memory lately. They were: "inching along, inching along , we'll get to Heaven by and by". I don't know if this was an old spiritual, but I just wondered if anyone else had heard such a song. Don't think it's my imagination. When we think of these words we know we are traveling the road of life at a slow pace. We do not know the years God has allotted us and we need to use them for Him and His Glory. You might say, "is that so important?" Yes, there are people who are looking at you daily. These people could be your children, neighbors, grandchildren, fellow workers or friends.

Our actions will speak much louder than words. We might talk about being a Christian all the time, but we should walk the walk, each day, showing our faith in Jesus Christ. Have you heard this, I can't hear what you say for seeing what you do?" When a person loses faith in us. as a Christian. talking about Jesus will mean nothing.

Read: Luke 14:34 & 35

What does power look like in the lives of people you know? Does it mean political or financial muscle? Jesus had all power, He could have called angels down from Heaven or done anything else on this earth. He chose to lay down His life for others, instead. The world would not view that kind of sacrifice as power, but when we look at the Savior, who He was, and why He came to the world, we see the most powerful person who ever walked on this earth. The beautiful truth is that we are looking at the power of Love, and that Love is beyond our understanding. How could Jesus, who owned everything, lay down His life for a sinner such as I? Yes, I said sinner, because we are all born in sin and until we accept Him as Savior and Lord, we remain in sin. When we accept Jesus, asking Him to come into our heart, forgive our sins, we are washed clean. That is, we become one of His forgiven ones.

Does that mean I will always do everything right? No, we are human beings, but when a converted person sins, the Holy Spirit will let him or her know immediately they need to ask forgiveness.

Read: John 10:25-29

We do not have to be a person that is famous, or one putting on a show so that others will look at us for God to use us. In fact, there are many people in the Bible that were only mentioned and these people were close to God. Let us think of Simeon, for instance, a man that very little was written about, and yet he took the Christ Child in his arms. To our knowledge he was not an ordained person or a leader, had no credentials or special authority. His name meant God hears. We see him as an example of a person who engaged in a lifetime of quiet prayer and watchfulness. He had faith that the Messiah would come, because

God had revealed this to him. He must have heard many rumors about the Messiah coming to set up His kingdom, about him coming in a great way, a rich king, and many other things yet, he quietly waited and trusted, and he knew who Jesus was when the Baby was placed in his arms. God honors a person who simply has a "just and devout" walk with him, as Simeon had. When we quietly get down to business with God, He will guide us in the way we should go.

Read: Luke 2:25-28

*J*esus knows all about our lives. He knows that life does not always seem fair to us. He knows we will have troubles, but we must remember He is the one who came to earth and went through all the trials and temptations we have each day. Because of His great sacrifice He invites us to come to Him and cast all our doubts, fears, anxiety and troubles on Him. When we were children the stories we read ended, "and they lived happily ever after". During those years children think of good things, romantic things as "The princess meets the prince, etc", but as we grow up we begin to face life as it really is. Of course we find happiness, but we never know what tomorrow will bring.

We do not know if it will bring sunshine or rain. We do know there is one that will walk with us in the sunshine and shelter us from the storms and that is Jesus. Every time the burdens get too heavy He will help each of us carry our load. The happy ever after is coming if we know Him as Savior and Lord. We have His Word on it and His Word is always true.

Read: 1st Peter 5:6 & 7

Do you remember the song, "How Beautiful Heaven must Be" or maybe you have never heard it. Heaven is more beautiful than our minds can comprehend. For each person who has accepted Jesus Christ it will be a place of joy and peace, no troubles, no tears and above all Jesus will be there. He said before He left He would prepare a place for us and we know His Word is true. The place for each of us will be perfect, with the river of life, clear as crystal, flowing from the throne of God and the Lamb, and the tree of life on either side of it. There will be streets of gold and no light will be needed there because the Lord God will be the light.

God showed His servant, John, all this and the vision was so awesome that John just fell on his face and worshiped. Let us realize that Jesus said He would prepare us a place and it will not be a cabin, but a place so beautiful we, in all of our imagination, cannot picture it.

Read: Revelation 21:18-21

*W*hat a Great God we serve! If things are going well for us now, in the future somewhere there is trouble and sorrow lurking. Should I dwell on this? Absolutely not, because there is a sure knowledge that I will never meet any need alone. Every time we have our heart wounded, find ourselves stranded or face great difficulty, God is there to bandage us, sooth, and help us find our way.

We, human beings. are not always faithful to Him, but our heavenly Father is always faithful to us. We have many testimonies from people like Catherine Marshall relating the assurance they have after great sorrows or losses. Although we do not know what sorrow is ahead for us, we can be confident God will be with us every step of the way, His help is available. Be thankful, trust God and depend on Him daily.

Read: Psalm 12:1-3

A person of faith in Jesus Christ living among non-believers can face many challenges.. They will be misunderstood and many times their values are looked upon as "old fashioned" or ignorant. This can be draining, because the Christian knows he or she has the values taken from God's Word. Even though we might live and work among unbelievers we do not have the kind of life the followers of Christ had in the Book of Acts. They were stoned, were plotted against and imprisoned for believing in Jesus. Their answer to this was prayer. They gathered together and prayed giving strength to each other. This is why we need to; meet together to worship today. We are to pray, and encourage our fellow Christians.

There are many myths in the world today and we are confronted with some of those. One of the most popular myths is this: "it doesn't matter what you believe, all are basically the same". Do not let yourself be fooled by this.

Read: Acts 4:12

What does it take for me to be pleasing to Jesus, be more like Him. Look at John the Baptist. He was an unexpected child, born to older parents, lived in the wilderness and wore strange clothing, and also ate strange food. He was on a mission for God, preparing the way for Jesus Christ entrance into society. He was not a rabbi of a large city synagogue and did not ride in a fine chariot. He was not invited to dine with leading citizens. Although he was different, people heard about him far and wide and they came to hear him. We find him speaking in a harsh way, and wonder why people came and why they listened to him. We never find him complimenting or "patting someone the head," but he told people they were sinners. In return, Jesus had nothing but praise for him. We see a man with a job to do for God and he finished it amid many trials and persecutions. Did his faith ever waiver? Yes, when he was in prison and Jesus did not go to him, he asked, "are you the one or should I seek another," so we see his humanity. Jesus did not go because John's job was finished on this earth and it was time for him to be with God, so he was beheaded.

Read: Matthew 11:7-11

Don't let Satan put a "guilt trip" on you and hinder your service for God. He would have you say, "I really messed up and God cannot use me now" "God wants nothing else to do with me, because I have disappointed Him." or people who have not been converted and have lived a life without God will excuse coming to Him by saying "I am too bad and have done too many bad things to be saved." Not true, these are lies of Satan to keep people from coming or depending upon the God of the universe.

When Jesus went to the cross He took the sins of the entire world upon Himself, so that we could be forgiven and inherit eternal life in Heaven. Do you belong to God, but have gotten out of His will, away from Him? What is the answer? Just go to Him in prayer, asking forgiveness and begin anew to live closer to Him. We do not ask forgiveness for a certain sin knowing we will commit it again tomorrow, but in sincerity turn, asking Jesus to forgive us. We know we are imperfect human beings, but we are to strive to please God at all times. He has a plan for your life just at He had one for Saul.

Read: Acts 9:13-15

God can do anything but fail! We might look at a man called Zacharias, an old man. When the angel appeared unto him and told him he was going to have a son he did not believe it. Why did he not believe? Because he was old and his wife was old and we know that humanly speaking people bear children in their younger years and there comes a time when this is not possible. Well, this time had come with Zacharias and Elizabeth and the news the angel was giving seemed impossible.

Is anything impossible with God? He has plans for your life and the only thing that will keep those plans from completion is YOU. We know how Zacharias was stricken dumb for his unbelief, and God had him to remain that way until he named John. God had a plan for Zacharias and Elizabeth and He also had a plan for the son who was to be born to them. John was to prepare the way for the Savior of the world and we see another birth that would be impossible to man, but we need to remember "With God all Things are possible."

Read: Mark 11:22-24

July

During these long hot days of summer, do you feel that nothing exciting ever happens to you? You might feel that you are in such a rut that every day is the same. Have we forgotten the excitement of serving the Lord Jesus Christ? We can become lazy and relaxed in our comfortable homes as David did making us targets for temptation or we can stay on out toes and stay excited about the blessings Jesus is giving us from day to day. You might have met someone who is famous or seen someone in the news and you saw the arrogance of that person and thought, "Look at me, I am a nobody" and you were feeling very inferior. How did Jesus handle things when He became known or we might say famous among some of the people? He did not choose to ride into town upon a prancing warhorse, but instead chose a donkey.

Our daily excitement is not to be measured by all the things around us, but by the peace of knowing we have a heavenly home and we have a wonderful Savior and Lord who will hear our prayer at any time of the day. A Christian should never be bored, because we have a friend who walks with us and listens to us at all times. Remember if you belong to Jesus you are a somebody, because you are a child of the King!

Read: Matthew 21:7-11

"Little is much when God is in it" God chose a childless immigrant couple, Abraham and Sarah, to found the Israelite nation and to witness to all nations. He chose Joseph, a favored son sold by his brothers to become a slave and He chose Moses to lead His people into the land of promise from Egypt. Stephen was chosen to help serve food to the widows and we find many others with jobs that seem to be of small account. When we look further into the scripture we see these people who were faithful to the calling of God were helping to carry out His will for all humanity.

Looking at some of the old Testament characters, we see the lineage of Jesus Christ who would come to earth later and died so that all men could be saved. We see Stephen's testimony being given to people for ages, giving encouragement to those who would give their lives for Christ when he said , " I see Jesus standing" He was telling the world, "I see Jesus waiting to receive me into heaven. These words would help further the early church. It matters not how much you can do for God or how many talents you have, but it does matter how we use what God has blessed us with.

Read: Mathew 14:17-21

Do we remember and believe that God keeps His promises? We hear promises from people every day. We see products that are guaranteed to last or be delivered at a certain time. Sometimes the promises are kept and at other times we are disappointed because someone has not kept his or her promise to us. This cannot happen with God. He kept His promise to Abraham and when we think of the promise He made of a Messiah who would come and save the people, we see it did not happen suddenly, but many years passed before Jesus came.

We are so time conscious we want to think God's time is the same as our time. We look at days and months and years, but to God a day is as a thousand years, and a thousand years is as one day. When the time was right Jesus came and died so that we could have eternal life. We must remember He said, "I will come again" and He will. We don't know when, but when His time is right this will happen just like He said.

Read: Romans 4:16-18

HAPPY FOURTH OF JULY! We look around us and listen to the news reports and realize that our country is not what God intended it to be. We have many who hate the flag and forget that much blood has been shed on battle fields to keep America free, hate God and cause discord constantly. We have corruption, greed and those in leadership who do not seem to care if we are a Christian Nation that our forefathers founded.

When we sing, "America the Beautiful" tears fill our eyes because we realize our Country is desperately needing a healing touch from God. Is there a solution? Yes, God gives us the solution in His Word. He says "if my people will, I will".

Read: 2nd Chronicles 7:14 and pray for our Country!

When we think of independence we are proud to say, "I'll do it myself, I depend on no-one else". This can be good to the extent that we know that we should never lose sight that we depend upon God. We might think we can do everything for ourselves but who gives us the ability to get up in the morning, who keeps our hearts beating and our bodies functioning? This tells me we can not be totally independent, but we are to do what we can, depending upon God for guidance. The majority in our Nation has allowed pride to come in just as the people when they thought to build the tower of Babel. They said, "let us build a tower that will reach into Heaven and become known for this feat". We look at this Scripture and see that God was so displeased with them He confounded their language and stopped the building of the tower and also the people scattered.

America has been blessed by God, becoming the greatest nation in the world and She has thought to do without God. Why do I say that? Because Christians are in a minority in this great country, now. We have been warned there would be a "falling away" from the Word of God and we see it each time we look at a news cast. Let us pray for our Country because we are still dependent upon the goodness of God and His blessings.

Read: 1st Timothy 6:17-19

*H*ow much do we need to pray? 1st Thessalonians, Chapter 5 tells us to rejoice and pray without ceasing. In other words, we are to be in a state of prayer at all times. He is not telling us to stay on our knees or have our heads bowed at all times. Elijah was a man talked about by James. This was a great prophet of God and he did not pray because he was a great man, but became a great man because he prayed. Do we have a lot in common with Elijah? He prayed fervently and kept praying with discipline. Elijah prayed an "effective" prayer or we would say he expected results. He did not allow sin to cloud his conversation with God, and we see him as a righteous man. He prayed specifically. We see him praying for a drought and then we see him praying for rain in accordance to God's Word.

Is there any reason a believer, today, cannot pray using the same principles he did? What would happen in our country if Christians began praying as Elijah prayed? We see in Deuteronomy, chapter 28 God tells His people He will make them the head and not the tail if they will listen and observe the law of God, not only to observe but to do them.

Read: James 5:13-18

❦ July 7 ❦

We had a message on low self esteem, yesterday and I have been thinking on it since. Have you ever felt worthless, unloved, all alone? Can we make our loved ones feel this way, especially our children? Do we build them us and tell them they can do anything with the help of the Heavenly Father? When a person has troubled times, he or she needs to go back to the day they received Jesus as Savior and Lord, and realize the Love He has for each of us. He loved each individual just the same, and there are no favorites. He shed His Precious Blood for anyone who will accept Him. Each soul is so important to Him He was willing to suffer and die for that soul to have eternal life. We find Elijah, the great prophet becoming discouraged and having a "pity party" thinking he was all alone and afraid of Jezebel because she had threatened his life. In 1st Kings 19, we find that God tells Elijah he is not alone but there are seven thousand more to help him.

Let us lift other people up and never put them down encouraging them that God is always there. A kind word, a touch, a smile, a compliment, might make the day for another much brighter. Parents, never put your children down by telling them they are not capable, but encourage them to be all they can be for God. Teach them the following verses.

Read: Philippians 4:8, 9 and 13

Christianity is characterized as the religion of Love. We know we are taught that God is Love and if we have Him in our heart we have love. But, it is very important not to take the emphasis of love to an unhealthy extreme. If in the name of love we accept the ideas or values in others which we know are against the Word of God, we open ourselves up to error. We are not to put our brains in neutral when it comes to matters of faith. John appeals for love repeatedly, but he also places great value on truth. He is not talking about the wishy-washy opinions of many people who change their minds and try to be politically correct all the time. John even tells us to test the spirit, to learn between truth and error. How do I know the truths in the Word of God? We are to study, as Paul advised Timothy to do, to show ourselves approved before God, so we will not be ashamed, as Christians, because we do not know the truth. John also advises Christians to stay away from those who deceive. They are leading people to believe lies instead of truth of God.

So, what is the answer to "love one another?" We are to love every human being alike. God made us all, but we are not to love or join them in the sins we know God is against. Any thing that is against God is to be hated, but the soul is to be loved, because Jesus died so that soul could be saved.

Read: 1st John 4:7-11

When other people look at you, what do they see? What image do you and I project? Is it a "don't care" attitude or an image of someone always looking to distrust another or maybe a "look at me, I am very important" image. Let us take note of ourselves, today. When Moses had an encounter with God, his face shined with such a bright glow, he had to wear a veil to hide the glory that shown from him. We, as believers, have God in the person of the Holy Spirit living within us and that is even closer than Moses was to God.

When we meet others they should see Jesus shining from us or do we veil Him with a mask of selfish ambition and worldly concerns? As we go about our daily routine we need to be aware that we are a testimony to someone and remember you and I might be the only Bible they will ever read. Will that person or persons see Jesus in us today?

Read: Matthew 5:14- 16

Looking at the news, today, we see destruction, suffering and deception on each news cast. We can look at these happenings and become very anxious. What is going to happen to our country? The disciples had the same fears and they looked for something solid and even commented to Jesus about the buildings, how great they were and the stones were solid. Jesus told them time would destroy the buildings. In other words Jesus was teaching things of this world are temporary and later He went into the end-time. He said there would be earthquakes, wars and famines. He was also teaching His followers they would face testing before councils, governors and kings. He warned of family members who would turn against each other.

Also Jesus warned about false prophets and people saying "Christ is over here or over there". Jesus is coming again! Many of the things He warned His disciples have happened in different countries. We, in America need to keep the faith. Christians should remember to pray for our Country that it will remain Christian. When others come into this country they should know they are coming into a Christian nation. We will never force anyone to believe as we do, but others should not try to force their beliefs on us.

Read: Mark 13:5-8

We are a people who naturally like to compete with others, but among Christians there is no place for competition, jealously or envy. We each have different abilities and whatever God has given us, He is pleased when we use it. Jesus knew His followers were in the grip of this common way of thinking, so He placed a child in front of them and affirmed that childlikeness is more desirable to God than competition. The disciples were vying to positions of power and prestige. We see this when we see the mother of James and John ask for the highest seats when Jesus comes into His kingdom. They were still looking for Him to set up His kingdom on earth, immediately. Jesus calls us to follow a different value system than the world's position which is competition and getting ahead by beating someone else. When we look around us, we see the field in which we are to work.

Instead of competition, we are to use compassion and care about others who are weak and forgotten. Do you know someone that needs a lift this morning, someone you need to help in the Name of Jesus?

Read: Luke 9:46-48

*F*or many people in the world today tension, worry, conflict, weariness and suffering have become commonplace. Then, they look at a television evangelist and are promised wealth, happiness and prosperity if they will send this or that to the speaker. Not true! There are others who teach when we accept Jesus Christ as Savior and Lord all our troubles will be over. Everything from that time on will be great. There are those who say faith will deliver us into a state of serenity and prosperity. Not true! These errors were not taught in God's Word.

Christians will have trails and tribulations, trouble on every hand, but the good news is this: Jesus has promised to be with us in our troubled times. Also the Christian has treasures money cannot buy. They have purity, kindness, sincere love, honor and good report. Each Christian has a peace that passeth understanding. In other words people do not know how a Christian can endure hardship and continue to worship God. We can never say we will not have stress if we serve Jesus Christ but we can take hope! We will enjoy heaven for eternity!

Read: John 14:27 & 28

"Tell me the story of Jesus, write on my heart every word" "Tell me the story of Jesus the sweetest that ever was heard". I was listening to a song last night that I do not remember hearing before and it was "tell me again about Jesus" or at least that was the message in the song. How many people might be hungry to hear the Word of God. Those who did not grow up hearing about Jesus and know they are missing something want to know about Jesus. We, as Christians, go to the house of God to be fed from the Word of God. Are we concerned about others who do not know about this opportunity?

Do we really care for those around us who need to know the sweetest story ever told? The Pastor might stand in the pulpit each Sunday and preach from God's Word, but what about those who are not present. Parents, Grandparents, what about the small ones who need to be taught about Jesus? We should never leave this job to someone else. We are responsible for teaching them. When Jesus told Peter to feed His sheep three times, He was putting emphasis on the importance of people being fed from the Word of God. God help us to teach and preach Your Word, daily, so there will not be a generation that has not heard.

Read: John 21:15-17

When we say love, today, we might be referring to many kinds of love. For instance, we will hear "I love this or that food", "I love that car", a certain brand of pizza or many other things. The word of love is thrown out to describe our liking for one thing or another. When we think of Jesus, we see a different kind of love. It is agape love, which is a unique kind of love. This is the kind of love that will cause a person to do good for another without expecting anything in return. This is the kind of love Jesus was talking about, when He recalled the greatest commandment.

Followers of Christ learn this kind of love, as God loves them first, He then commands them to love others. This kind of love enables us to love by choice rather than just emotion or senses and to sustain our love even in the face of hostility or rejection. Christians, let us look around and see who needs this kind of compassion, this kind of grace? As the song says, "The Love of God, how rich and Pure"...It is more marvelous than we can imagine and the beautiful thing is this, "It shall forever more endure".

Read: Matthew 22:37-40

As we study the Scripture, we see Jesus heading south with His disciples from Galilee and going through Samaria. The Jewish people commonly bypassed Samaria because of prejudice. The Samaritans were a people who had been born from captured Jews, making them half-breeds. Jesus chose this route deliberately as if to give His disciples a good lesson.

The conflict erupted in the first village they entered because the foreigners did not want Jesus and His followers there, nor did the disciples want to be there. Neither group could see past the ethnic identity of the other. The response, by the disciples, actually shows how destructive hatred and bitterness can be. It actually caused them, Jesus' own followers, to distort the Scriptures. They wanted to call down fire from heaven, as Elijah did, but they did not say that Elijah called down fire from Heaven to destroy the sacrifice and not the people. Elijah was not praying for God to punish the people, but to show His great power. Jesus rebuked His disciples and actually let them know the spirit of evil was causing them to think this way. They were supposed to be there to save and not destroy the people.

Read: John 9:51-56 and John 3:17

We pray and pray for a beloved to be healed physically. Are we praying for selfish reasons? Are we praying to keep this person on earth with us, because we enjoy their presence? There are many times when God will reach down and heal because He has more for that person to do on earth, but there are time He heals by taking the person to Heaven. There, he or she will have a perfect body, free from pain. God has a plan and the human mind cannot understand God's plan.

When Stephen was stoned, we see him telling those around him, "I see Jesus standing at the Father's right hand". This tells us God allowed Stephen to see that Jesus was waiting to receive him. We know the Scripture tells us in Mark Chapter 16:19 that Jesus sat at the Father's right hand when He ascended. But He is standing to receive this Christian allowing him the joy of seeing Him. God allowed Stephen to be stoned to further His work on earth and for a testimony to all those around, but in the midst of this Stephen received the blessing of seeing Jesus waiting for him.

Read: Acts 7:54-56 & 8:4

People will not forget sin, but God does. When we ask a person to forgive us they might say they do, but as soon as we have a disagreement this sin will be unpacked, aired and shaken about again. The Word of God tells us that when we repent with a sincere and contrite heart, God will forgive and cast our sins as far away as the East is from the West. This means our sins are gone and can be found no more. The slate has been wiped clean, because God doesn't keep records of forgiven sins. You are not to let Satan bring to your mind past mistakes and sins when God has forgiven you of them. This is one of his ploys. If he can make you miserable, regretting the past, he will do so.

A person who has been converted, forgiven by God, is to be a happy person because the load of sin is gone and they have a wonderful Savior who has gone back to Heaven to prepare them a place, eternally. Remember no person's scorecard matters when your record has been cleared with God.

Read: Psalm 103:8-12

*J*ust as I posted my devotion, yesterday, the internet went down and the post did not get on. Sorry about that, but we know Satan would defeat us if we were to become discouraged, so today we are going to talk about computers. One way to set up a network is to have a central computer for storage and communication functions. This is similar to the situation Jesus described in His image of the vine and the branches. Jesus is the key. Just like the central processing unit of a computer, He provides life, direction and commands for His followers, for those of us "on line."

In order for us to use the features of the network, we must remain attached to the network and if we "sign off" communication is broken. So it is with the Christian's relationship with Jesus Christ. If we allow Satan to lure us into the sins that will easily beset us, we will not be able to have a clear line of prayer or we will say communication with Jesus. Until we pray for forgiveness, and forgive others Jesus will not hear us when we pray. Having unforgiven sins creates a barrier between us and the heavenly Father. In the sample prayer Jesus gave His disciples we find, "forgive us as we forgive others".

Read: Luke 17:2-4

*T*he fears of this life, what are they? Are people afraid of poverty, losing all our earthly possessions? God gives us these material things to be used and we should never think "I did it myself" because He gave each of us the strength to get up in the morning and earn the things we enjoy. We are taught to look at the ant and see her working, and this tells us we are to work as long as we can for our needs.

We, as Christians, when we do what we are able to do, should not worry because God has promised He will take care of our NEEDS. So, our fear should not be poverty, but we should fear God. This is not the cringing fear that keeps us wallowing in anxiety, but a respect for who God is. He is the One who holds the ultimate power, the Giver of life, The Great I Am. When we have a balanced view of God, it puts our thinking in a proper framework. With this balanced view we will see everything in relation to God's holiness, righteousness and love. We might have losses, physical threats and violence to deal with, but we dare not ignore the One who controls our eternal destiny.

Read Proverbs 1:7 & Luke 12:13-15

I hope everyone has a wonderful week, as you continue to worship the King of Kings. How wonderful to serve a God who formed us and understands all our weakness and still has grace filled plans for us. We are not to let our past, not even yesterday dictate our future but instead we are to let His past, His perfect atonement for our sins on the cross tell us who we are and what He would have us do for Him.

God has plans for each life and even though we fail Him many times, He will forgive us and use us to glorify Him and carry out His plans. This we must remember: He can and will use you for His purpose, but each person has to let Him in. Remember the picture we have all seen many times of Jesus standing at the door knocking? He is waiting for each of us to invite Him in and ask Him to take control of our life. God even had plans for Saul, the Christian persecutor.

Read: Acts 9:13-16

$\mathcal{A}$ sermon our Pastor gave us recently was so fitting for each Christian and I have been thinking on it, since. It was about regret. There is no person who if and when he or she thinks back. as Satan would have us do, does not regret things he or she has done or the things that have been left undone in the past. The prime examples given us in the sermon were Peter and Saul. I have thought of Peter many times. Because of fear, he denied the Lord three times just as Jesus said he would. But he had declared he would be with the Savior through anything. How he must have felt when Jesus looked at Him after his denial. We see Saul, a person who persecuted Christians, had them dragged out and thrown in prison, beaten or killed. I am sure he had many regrets when Jesus stepped in, changed his name and saved him for service in the mission field.

The conclusion of the entire matter is this: When a person accepts Jesus, it doesn't matter what he or she has done in the past. It doesn't matter what he or she has left undone, all is forgiven and cast as far from that person at the east to the west. We are not to let Satan dredge up things from our past and bring those regrets to haunt us, because they are gone and forgotten. That is the reason Jesus shed His Blood for us. By His Blood we are washed clean.

Read: Psalm 103:10-12

*D*o you face times in your life when you feel your faith waning? You have prayed and prayed about something or someone and nothing has happened. Where is God during these times? He is there all the time. When Lazarus was so ill, his sisters knew if Jesus would come he would be healed, but Jesus did not come when they thought He should and they both told him, "If you had been here our brother would not have died". God's plan was different from man's plan. Lazarus was to be raised to show the glory of God and for people to see who Jesus was. We must realize we do not understand God's plans, but we also we must realize His plans are perfect.

When the Angel told Abraham that Sarah was to have a son in her old age, she laughed thinking this was impossible, but in Genesis 18:14 the angel asked her, "Is anything too hard for the Lord". In Isaiah chapter 40, verses 28 and 29 we are told that God never faints, never grows weary, and gives power to the weak.

When we feel ourselves growing weak and feeling as though we want to "give up" because of heartache and trouble, let us remember that God has a plan for each life. Depend on Him, even though you do not see the answer to your prayer quickly. Remember, God is there.

Read: Ephesians 3:19 & 20

*H*ow often do we see people afraid of what might happen in the future? Do you say, "I would begin this or that", but I am afraid I will not be able to finish it".? Have you talked to God about these things? The things Satan has us to become afraid of, are the things that usually do not happen. When we worry we are wasting our time and cannot be the person God would have us be. Let us set our minds on things we know are going to happen.

We know we will see our Savior face to face when we die. We know He has told us He will be with us in whatever trouble or trial we have. We know He is coming again, because we know He keeps His promises. We know He will hear and answer our prayers in His time and in His way. We know the answer might not be what we expect because He does not always say yes, because there are many times we do not know what we are asking for.

We know when we tell someone about Him, His Word will not return void, seeds were planted to grow at a later date. Let us cast our fears on Jesus.

Read: 1st Peter 5:6-8

*I*s Jesus really Lord of all in your life? Do we make Him Lord of only the things we dedicate to Him or do we realize He is Lord of everything and everyone. Let us look at the Pharisees. Their law of the Sabbath was so important to them, they could not accept Jesus and His disciples gathering a handful of grain and eating it on the Sabbath day. To them Jesus was violating their extreme view of resting on this day.

Jesus added to their consternation by reminding them of King David and how he entered the temple and ate the ceremonial showbread. Jesus was establishing Himself as Lord of the Sabbath Day and in fact of all creation. He, as Lord, was free to determine what was permissible and He would not let the Pharisees box Him in to their way of way of saying what was "sacred" and what was "secular". When we think of this, we need to search ourselves. In what areas of our lives do we try to keep Jesus from being Lord? Do we try to limit His authority in order to preserve our own ideas?

Read: Luke 6:1-5

John the Baptist was a great teacher. Oh, I know when we look at how he talked to people and how he lived to himself, we say, "how could he have been a great teacher, he had a terrible personality?" John came to this earth to do a job and he did it well. Oh yes, he became discouraged when he was in prison and Jesus did not come. We hear his question to Jesus, "are you the one or should I look for another"? In this question we see discouragement, because he knew Jesus was in the area. John was not a jealous person, afraid that someone would usurp his authority or popularity. He said "Jesus must increase and I must decrease."

God's plan for this servant was to prepare the way for Jesus and this he did. He told people he was not the Bridegroom but a friend of the Bridegroom. He was talking about the children of God being the bride of Christ. John followed God and completed his mission and when his mission was completed God allowed him to be killed. He had a home in heaven. We must remember God has a plan for each of us and when it is completed we have a heavenly home.

Read: John 3:27-30

We must have a determination to stay with Jesus even amid troubles and trials. In the Scriptures we see Zacchaeus was so determined to see Jesus he climbed into a tree. The woman who had the issue of blood for so many years was determined if she could just get to Him, Jesus would heal her. David was determined to show the power of God when he went against a giant with a sling and stones. When we see the followers of Christ in Acts and see the persecutions they endured for God, and there must have been some who gave up, but there were those who kept serving and telling others. All these have testimonies of staying, no matter the cost, and that is why we have God's Word today.

Through the ages there have been many determined Christians to hold Jesus up to a dying world. During this time in which we live, we realize Christians are becoming a minority. Let us ask God to give us the strength to serve Him, no matter the circumstances. Let us remain determined to follow Christ at all cost.

Read: Acts 5:40-42

As we look into God's Word we might stand in awe of the plan that God had for each of us from the beginning. We know when we look at John 1:1 that the Word, (Jesus) has been with God from the beginning. The garden of Eden was a perfect place but sin entered and from that time people have been tempted by Satan to disobey God. Then we see, when we study the Word, that Satan tried to destroy everyone he knew to be in the lineage from which Christ would come.

Of course we also see God preserving this lineage from Seth through the Exodus and we see David, a man after God's own heart, giving in to the temptations of Satan. We also see in the Psalms how unhappy he was until he asked God to restore unto him the Joy of God's salvation, being sorry for his sins. Satan did his best to keep the Messiah, prophesied in Isaiah, Jeremiah, Micah, Psalms and other prophets from the earth. There were many innocent baby boys killed by Herod, trying to get to Jesus. There is never a doubt that God's plan is perfect and will be completed. Satan could not stop it and Jesus was born, grew up among people, was tempted by Satan and remained the perfect sacrifice for each of us. How beautiful is the plan of God!

Read: Isaiah 53:2-6

Are you having a "pity party"? Yes, Christians, because of things that happen in their lives, can begin feeling sorry for themselves. Their thinking is this: "I have mistreated by others and I have had sorrows and God has not answered the many prayers I have prayed". "He seems to have deserted me, because when I pray I am not sure He even listens, so I am ready to give up." All of these ideas, which come from Satan, are wrong. God is still on His throne and He does know about your troubles and sorrows. He answers prayer, but not in the time and way we think He should. Really, we try to out think God and this is impossible. We have the story of Elijah and the message he received from Jezebel. After all the prophets of Baal were slain, she swore to kill Elijah and we find Elijah, the great prophet running for his life. He had a great pity party, sitting under a juniper tree he even asked God to kill him. When Elijah went to dwell in a cave, God came to him and asked him what he was doing there and his answer was, "I am the only one left and they seek my face" In other words he was telling the angel people were looking for him to kill him.

God does not listen to these words of discouragement but tells His people to "go" as He did Elijah. You have many Christian brothers and sisters to encourage and pray for you. Stephen in all his persecution had no pity party, but prayed "Father forgive them" and saw Jesus as he was dying.

Read: Acts 7:54-60

We. as Christians, need to realize we have two ways to communicate. One way is our actions. We are seen by others each day, hourly, and those who live with us and work with us are influenced by out attitudes and actions. The other way is the words we speak. What kind of language do you use each day? Do you think vulgar words will make you more popular? Who will you impress with this kind of language and what will be the impression you leave?

There is an old saying, "sticks and stones may break my bones, but words can never hurt me." This is wrong. Words can hurt a person for a lifetime. Parents might carelessly call one of their children stupid and that child will have the impression that he or she is stupid and incapable the rest of their life. Beware of repeating things you have heard. Gossip has hurt, even killed many people. When we look into the Scripture we find Peter speaking before he was thinking. He even told the Lord he would follow Him to the end and we see him deny even knowing Jesus. " Lord, help us control our tongues and if we can't say something good, help us to say nothing at all, and help us to think before we speak." "Help us to keep our thoughts centered on you and see the good in others."

Read: James 3:7-11

Do you stagger under a heavy load of expectation that you should bring your friends, family and those you know to Christ? Do you feel guilty because you cannot get them to listen, to believe God's Word? We are only responsible for your every day living and influence on others. We cannot draw them to Jesus. While He was explaining about the Kingdom of God, Jesus declares that only God can draw a person to Him. You will find this in John 6:44.

So the responsibility of conversion clearly belongs to the Father, but does not relieve us of the responsibility of giving evidence of how God has worked in our lives and how He is still working in our lives as we grow to become stronger Christians. We are to offer clear, truthful, information about the gospel when we have the opportunity. We can invite others to believe in the one who shed His precious blood so that each person has a chance to go to a home in heaven when he or she dies. So, we are to relax, live in faith, talk about it and offer to help others understand. But the dynamic conversion is from God above. We find Jesus teaching that He, only, was the Bread of life.

Read: John 6:63-66

In the first few verses of John we find a reminder that Jesus is the Word. Word is a Greek term meaning a thought expressed. When we think of it we see that Jesus is the human expression of God. John uses the metaphors as the Light and the Flesh. We see Jesus in the flesh when we read, "and He became Flesh and dwelt among us." We know to see Jesus is to see God and to know Jesus is to experience God's grace and truth. The Grace, unmerited favor, of God is the Gospel. Jesus came to this earth, grew up in a poor home, and was tempted in all ways as we are, and because of the great Love of God went to the cross and died so that each person would have a chance to be saved from an eternal hell. This is God's Grace.

The unmerited favor means we have done nothing to deserve Jesus dying for us, but He did it all. We might think of being in the bondage of sin or being held in the prison of sin, and Jesus paid our fine. Every person who accepts Him is released, because of what He did for us. Jesus was able to look down through the ages and see each of us and know that we needed the choice of coming to Him, or we each would be doomed.

Read: John 1:14-18

August

*W*hen we look in the Book of Genesis we see a city destroyed because of evil. We also see, as the angels led Mrs. Lot out with her husband and two daughters, she had her mind on those things she had left behind. She had been warned not to look back, not to long for the way of life that displeased God, but when she did not listen to the warning she was destroyed. The things she had left behind were more important to her than obeying God. Jesus warned His disciples to remember her When He gave this warning to His disciples He was telling them about His second coming. He promised to return and He will come back.

We hear people say this, "I have been hearing all my life that Jesus is coming again, and He has not come." He did not tell us the time, but the timing is in the hands of God and we must remember that a thousand years is as a day with the Lord. When we think of this in God's time table, Jesus hasn't been gone long. Instead of thinking we are able to know when Jesus is coming we just each need to be ready.

Read: Matthew 25:31-34 and verse 41

When a person is converted, he or she is considered a "babe" in Christ. The meaning of this is the amount that person has to learn to mature as a Christian. An older Christian can also remember some of these seasoned lessons taught to young Timothy by Paul. When a person is saved, he or she might think everything will be easy for the rest of their life. The number one lesson is this: We live in a broken world and tough times will come. The next lesson is the lesson of thankfulness.

All good and perfect gifts come from God, let us thank Him for all our blessings. And a very important advise to remember is this: Don't forget to assemble with others to affirm the truth with those who share your faith. Avoid getting caught up in folk lore and superstitions, make sure you search out the truth from God's Word. When you are around a skeptic, do not listen but turn your thoughts to the basics like the love of Christ, a conversation that will help others, and purity of mind. The last lesson I will mention is this: We should work on our own abilities and skills because these abilities are given us by God and as His servants we should use them for His Glory.

Read: 1st Timothy 4:1-3 & 7

*I*n our society we think of power as being able to accomplish a number of things. We hear that a person is a powerful person because he or she has a lot of money or they are popular politically. A person could even be called powerful if the individual is a famous movie star or writer. When Jesus was describing His power he was telling the people it all came from God. Do we stop to realize that God is above all, and in control of all circumstances?

Are we guilty of living from day to day without thanking Him for the blessings He gives us? The Scriptures tell us all good and perfect gifts come from Father God. We look into the Old Testament and see the power given individuals like Elijah and Elisha as they gave the people prophesy from God. We see the nation Israel. a nation God blessed by giving them their land, and we also see when they disobeyed Him the power of God was taken from them and they even became slaves in Egypt for forty years. So the conclusion is this: God gives power and He takes it away according to His Will.

Read: John 10:17 & 18

How sad it was that humanity would not accept Jesus as the Messiah, the Savior of the world! All the Israelite boys had been taught that the Messiah would come and people were looking for a king to come and establish a rich kingdom. When this child was born in a very poor place and raised by a poor carpenter, with no show of worldly wealth, Jesus was not recognized. Even though He did many miracles with His final one being the raising of Lazarus, Jesus was never accepted as the Son of God who had come to take away the sin of the world. We see Him left after the Passover period by Joseph and Mary and telling them, when they returned for Him, He had to be about His Father's business. Yes, He had some followers, twelve who were His disciples and even they did not understand that He was not going to set up His kingdom at this time.

How alone He must have felt when he prayed in the garden. His heart must have been broken to see His trusted disciples sleeping instead of watching for Him. He had all the human feelings we do and we must understand how much He suffered in His human body for us. The beautiful part of all this is: He defeated Satan on the Cross when He died so that we might have eternal life. His promise to us, "I go to prepare a place for you and I will come again and receive you to Myself."

Read: John 12:37 & 38 and John 12:42 & 43

*W*hen we were children and our parents went into town we would eagerly await their return and the first thing asked was, "did you bring me anything?" Instead of looking into the dad or mother's face and saying "I love you" the human part of a person is thinking of themselves. When a person requests that you do something for them, is your first thought, "what's in it for me"? Have we grown up in a selfish society? Jesus never once showed this kind of attitude. In fact, He knew that His future was the giving of Himself on the Cross for the sins of all people. He humbly and willingly followed God's will and endured the suffering so that we could all be forgiven. Jesus knew how unloving the human could be. He heard the mother of two of His disciples ask for the highest seats in His kingdom.

He knew He was betrayed for a few pieces of silver and He also saw how unthankful the nine lepers were when just one came back to thank Him. When we go to the Lord in prayer, do we seek His Face because we love Him or do we selfishly seek His Hand for our wants and desires? If we would learn to seek His Face with thankfulness and love, wanting His Will, not ours, that would be enough.

Read: Matthew 6:31-34

We read of leaven in the Bible and we know it is the substance that makes dough rise. Today we purchase yeast to make our rolls or bread rise. Why was Jesus so displeased with the perception of the disciples when He told them to beware of the leaven of the Pharisees and Herod? The disciples could not understand that He wasn't talking about bread. He reminded them of the feeding of the five thousand and how the bread was multiplied and how they gathered up twelve baskets of left-over fragments. The message to the disciples was the growth of evil. Jesus wanted them to see the false teachings of the Pharisees would grow and more and more people would believe them. Herod wanted people to believe he was a God and Jesus knew that also would grow and many people would believe it.

Let us think of yeast. It is a fungus that can make a lump of dough rise, ferment liquids into alcohol and it can also cause terrible infections. How many beliefs have we seen spread in our society, that have grown at great speed. Scriptures have been turned to make people feel good instead of making them realize we all need Jesus Christ in our lives. One of these errors is this: "there are many ways to Heaven" We know this is not true because Jesus said, "I am the way, the truth and the light, no man cometh to the Father but by me.

Read: John 14:6 & Mark 8:15

A beautiful illustration in the Bible is given in the Book of Jeremiah. God told Jeremiah to go down to the potter's house and there he showed him how the potter could take a piece of clay and mold it. Of course, the entire message was about a nation. We might look at this and think of individuals. We are created out of the dust of the ground, so let us call ourselves the lump of clay. God has a plan for each life, but many times the individual rebels and wants to go his or her own way. This is the story of the young man who wanted his inheritance early and went his way, spending all his goods and ending up eating with the pigs. The way he could make his life right again was returning to the Father and confessing his sins.

When we rebel, we are a marred piece of clay, but the Master Potter can remold us. If our nation will turn to God, as Jeremiah was calling Israel to do, God will make us, once again, a nation that can be called Christian. Think of the Potter throwing the piece of clay back on the wheel, spinning and shaping it to His will. We suffer the consequences of our actions, but returning to God is worth everything becau he repairs our lives.

Read: Jeremiah 18:1-4 & 8

*I*f you have something against a Christian Brother or Sister, something is wrong, not with them, but with you. Confusion in our churches is demonic. I have seen people who have accepted Christ and are still a "babe" or we would say a young Christian, wanting to grow in the admonition of the Lord and along comes someone with a chip on his or her shoulder and a gossip that is led by Satan and destroys all the young believers confidence in people of God. Jesus told us to love each other and that is to love each other with Christian Love. The kind of love that prays for each other, the kind of love that forgives mistakes, the kind of love that will lift a person up and not tear him or her down. This kind of love in a Church shows the love of Christ to those who are outside looking in. This kind of love will make others want to accept Jesus Christ.

If you have aught against a brother or sister, go to the person and ask forgiveness, and make things right. If Jesus asked God to forgive the treatment He received, surely we can forgive little things. Do you love the Lord, and want to be the kind of influence you should be?

Read: John 13:34 & 35

*T*here was a song my children sang years ago, "Do you really care". The message is plain. Do we focus on ourselves and how inconvenient it is to help with this or that in our church, or to help another in need, or to teach God's Word"? When we really care we will not focus on ourselves or any sacrifice we must make to help someone. The sacrifice becomes a part of our activity and is wrapped up in the love we have for God.

We really need to forget ourselves and ask God what He would have us do, today. Is Jesus asking you to really care? We are not to do something because we feel pressured, or guilty. Everything is to be done because we are willing to obey God. When our attitude and actions become thus, we forget our selfishness and serve Him, God in Heaven smiles and our joy will overflow.

Read: Romans 12:1 and look at the parable Jesus gave in Luke 10:30-37

*T*his is the day the Lord hath made, let us rejoice and be glad in it. Have you thought of all your blessings this morning? Do you appreciate the things God gives you enough to want to go to His house and worship him? There are times when we are physically unable to assemble ourselves with fellow Christians and if is our usual way, we know we have missed something all the following week. There is a satisfaction in worshiping God with fellow believers and this is why we are told in the Scriptures not to forsake the assembling of ourselves together.

God knows we need the fellowship of other believers, the encouragement and we need the time apart to worship Him. Sure, we are able to worship at home, watch a minister on TV, and think about the blessings God has given us, but it isn't the same. If you are physically able do not miss the privilege of worshiping God today. Listen to the news and you will hear of many Christians who have fled to the mountains, fearing for their lives and knowing they might starve or be killed for believing in God. They cannot gather to worship him.

Read: James 1:17

Did you notice all the beauty around you, this morning? The beautiful sunrise or rain to help things to grow. We have been given years, and sometimes they seem so few, to enjoy all the beauty God has given us. When we look at a baby smile, see a beautiful flower, trees that are ready to turn from gold to brown, stars at night, how blessed we are. Let us not set our sights on material things so much we miss these things. Also, let us not lose sight of the time we may be with our family and loved ones.

Time is so precious and we need to use it wisely. Yes, we need to work to earn a living, but we also need to take the time to enjoy all the blessings God has given us. Why should I set my heart and sight on material things, when I am going to die one day and leave them. We will carry to Heaven what we have done for Jesus, for His glory, not for the praise of man. We will leave behind the memories of what we have done for Jesus, the testimony, those we have influenced for His kingdom.

Read: 1st Timothy 6:17

*H*ave you thought of a Christian being like a plant? If a plant is not watered (Jesus said, "I will give you water and you will never thirst again) and fed plant food (Bread of Life) the plant will dry up and become useless. The same thing is true with a Christian. If he or she does not learn from God's Word and pray for the strength that will come from God, they will not grow. That person will not be able to take part in a conversation about God's Word or answer questions that might be asked them. That was the reason Paul told Timothy to study to show himself approved, rightly dividing the Word of God, so he would not be ashamed.

The woman at the well asked Jesus to give her the living water and we know this is forgiveness or we will say she asked for salvation. After a person accepts Jesus as Savior and Lord, the need is to learn more about Him, and that can only be done with listening to sermons, teaching, prayer and study of God's Word. A Christian, just like a plant, has his or her roots planted and those roots are in Jesus. Spend time alone with Him. Ask for wisdom as you study His Word and He will grant your wishes. Remember Christ is the vine and we are branches.

Read: John 15:1-4

*T*he old saying you have heard from childhood is this, "actions speak louder than words." This is absolutely true. The things you do and the attitude you show to others everyday will tell them know if you are living as a Christian. You have someone who watches you to see if you are living by the Christian standards you proclaim. I have an article that was written by my mother and it is about a little old lady in a long black dress sitting at worship. Mother was a small child and observed the way the lady worshiped God. She saw the sincere look on her face and the adoration as she listened to the message that day. The child did not remember the pastor's message, but she did remember the actions of the lady.

You are an influence to someone. That someone could be a child, a person trying to decide if they should follow Jesus, or someone who has been a friend for a long time and they have confidence in what you say. But, if your language and actions are ungodly, the person loses that confidence and your influence is as salt that has lost its flavor and is no good. Walk your Talk!

Read: Matthew 5:13-16

*W*hen we choose to follow Jesus or in the Bible we see this is called to be a disciple, there is a cost, and there are also many, many blessings. Some of the costs of serving Jesus are these: We must serve Him before all others. In other words Jesus is to be first in our lives. Sometimes our interest must be put on hold in order to do what we know Jesus would have us do. We, who follow Christ, must be fully aware of who we are and what Christ has equipped us to do. We need to know when Christ calls us to a job for Him, He will also equip us to do it. We are not to act as Moses did when He told God He could not speak to the Pharaoh.

We know God would have enabled him but because of him not depending on God, his brother was made his speaker. We must also have the courage and faith to know that Jesus walks with us as we face different issues in our lives. Let us stand up the way a Christian should, speak up and live a life that will be pleasing to God. The pay is out of this world! (Heaven)

Read: Matthew 12:28-30

*J*esus said, "Come unto me all ye who are heavy laden and I will give you rest". He is telling each of us that we will have burdens in this life. The load will become heavy, many times, because we will be troubled and sorrowful, but Jesus knows all that. He lived on this earth and was persecuted, had friends turn against Him, even to the point of saying they did not know Him. As the Scripture predicted He was despised and He was wounded for our sins. (Isaiah 53: 2-5) He doesn't promise we won't have burdens but He promises to help us carry our burdens.

Whatever you have that is a great burden to you today, turn to Jesus and ask Him to help you carry it. He will give you the peace inside that other people will not understand. The peace He gives is the assurance that He is with you and will walk with you and as we read in the poem of "Footprints" When you are unable to travel the road, He will carry you.

Read: Matthew 11:28-30

Do you remember the song, which we do not hear today, "How Beautiful Heaven must be." I do not know if that is the correct title, but I have been thinking about the words therein. When we think of Heaven, we cannot imagine the beauty there. When Jesus said He would prepare a place for us, His preparation has endless beauty. Let us think of twelve gates and each of them a great pearl. The wall of the city is made up of precious stones and the street is pure gold, so pure it is as transparent glass.

What a vision God gave John! We see there is no temple or most of us would say church, there. The reason for this is because the Lord God Himself will be the temple. No light will be needed, because He is the light. When I read the description of Heaven, it is a great thrill, because I know this will be the eternal home of each of us who have accepted Jesus Christ as Savior and Lord.

Read: Revelation: 21:18-23

*P*aul admonishes Christians to live peaceably with those around us. in Colossians Chapter 3, Verse 13. How can we do this when there is conflict all around us? Number one is refusing to take offence when others hurt us. Next, we are not to get entangled in the affairs of others and then we should humbly accept the circumstances God sends us for our good, instead of arising each morning to grumble through the day about this or that. When we do not live peaceably with others and habitually grumble, people around us do not see a Christian walking with God. Instead they see an unhappy person that no other can please, a person who is away from God.

A person that no one wants to stay near. We might hear this from a child: "When I grow up I don't want to be like him or her". A sad person, indeed, is one that people try to avoid in order to be with happier people. Let us take inventory, today. What kind of Christian am I? Do I build others up or am I negative in my talk and thinking so they want to stay away?

Read: Matthew 5:9-12

God has a plan for my life and your life. We do not always see how things are going to work out when things seem to be so far from what we had thought God wanted us to do. Look into the Scripture and see how God worked in different lives to bring His plans about for good. Jonah did not want to do what God called him to do and tried to run away, but God used a storm and a fish to make him preach where he was supposed to preach. Joseph's brothers sold him into slavery and we can imagine how Joseph felt.

God had given him dreams and they foretold his family bowing down to him. Many times bad things happen in our lives and they tend to strengthen us to do and be what God has planned for us all the time. Do we ask God to show us His will for our lives? When we pray do we ask His will to be done? If we do not know God's will for our life, will we pray for Him to show us?

Read: Jeremiah 29:11-13

"Give me liberty or give me death" We remember Patrick Henry from our history books. People desire liberty, but there is only one way for us to have true liberty and that is liberty in Jesus Christ. He provided forgiveness so we would could be freed from the bondage of sin. Not only that, but Jesus Christ has provided renewal for all of our life. Second Corinthians tells us this: "If any man (Person) be in Christ old things pass away, all things become new." 2nd Cor. 5: 17. Also He will give us the power and strength to carry out His work. His promise was, "Ye shall receive power, the power to witness of me". He also promised to give a comforter which is the Holy Spirit. He said, "I must go away but I will not leave you comfortless."

The Holy Spirit comes to dwell within each person who accepts Jesus as Savior and Lord. Jesus has established guidelines for proper conduct for His followers. We, who belong to Christ shall not hate our brother because this hate will cause us to walk in darkness. We need to remember Christ came for each soul on this earth and each one has a choice to accept Him or reject Him.

Read: 1st John: 2:9 & 10

What does power look like or mean to you? Does it mean looking at someone who can get things done politically? Does it mean having control over others? Does it mean how much money a person has? We have heard many times that money can buy anything. But, can money and all the political power buy happiness. What about popularity? Even though someone might be an idol to many people, this does not call for happiness. We know that Jesus was all powerful.

He could have called ten thousand angel to protect Him from the cross, but He used His power to lay down His life for you and me. The world will not view this kind of sacrifice as power, but we as Christians know this was the profound power of love. "For God so loved the world He gave His only Begotten Son, that any one who would believe in Him might have eternal life." Jesus was powerful enough to do something that no other could do.

Read: Acts 9:13-16

*W*hen you think of the calling of God on your life, how do you perceive it? What and how do I know the calling of God? In the Scriptures we find Jesus calling people to follow Him. The twelve disciples were in different places and doing different things when Jesus passed by. He called the poor working fishermen and the tax collector. Jesus makes no difference in the people He calls. He sends out the call to everyone, " I am the way the truth and the life, no man comes to the Father, but by me". "Come unto me and I will give you rest." "Take my yoke upon you and learn of me."

When a person is willing to follow Christ, He will put them into the place of service He has for them. Paul had a call from God to go to the Gentiles and become a great Missionary. Yes, we are all equal with God, but He has different positions we are apt to fill. He has people for everything that is needed in His Kingdom's work. Preachers, Teachers, Missionaries, Singers, those talented in music. We could go on and on about all the positions to be filled.

Read: Matthew 11:28-30

The first time Jesus sent His disciples out he told them to carry nothing. No sword, and no purse. They were to go and tell those they came in contact with the gospel. They were to tell them about Jesus. Today, we should take the warning of Jesus to heart when He warned to watch out for covetousness or we might say greed. When a person thinks he or she has saved enough funds and are set for life they tend to depend on themselves and forget God. This can be a dangerous thing in our lives.

We live in a society that looks at wealth, status and power, alas, God is left out of the equation. Whatever we have gained, materially, will not go with us when we die. We came into the world with nothing and we will leave this world the same.

Does this mean I am not to work? Certainly not, the Bible tells us to look at the ant and when we do we will see a working insect always on the move. We are not to put anything before God. God means for us to work and leave the rest to Him. Read the parable Jesus gave of the rich man and notice how many times he says "I" in his planning, leaving God out.

Read: Luke 12:16-21

*O*f all that Jesus did, John was a writer determined to show He was the Son of the living God and that believing, a person would have life in His name. The works done by Jesus clearly shows who He was and why He came to earth. A person cannot live without water and bread so Jesus turned the water into wine showing He was the source of life, and fed five thousand people with five barley loaves and two fish showing He was the bread of life. He showed all humanity He was Master over time when he healed the man at the pool of Bethesda who had not been able to walk for a long time. He walked on water showing He was Master of nature, and healed a man who was blind, showing He was the Master of light.

Just as that man had walked in darkness a person who has not accepted Jesus walks in darkness. He or she does not know what Jesus did for each of us, until they accept and learn of Him. We who know Him, know He is the light of the world. John gives the account of Lazarus who had been buried for four days. When Jesus came to the devoted sister, Mary, He wept showing His compassion for us in our troubles. But then we see the greatest gift of all demonstrated when He raised Lazarus. When He comes back, the dead in Christ will rise first and all that remain will be caught up to live with Him.

Read: John 14:1-3

God wants us to trust in His power. When Gideon was threshing wheat and hiding it because they were overtaken by the Midianites, and he had to hide to keep the wheat and not have them force it from him, an angel came to him and gave him a call from God. The call was to get up and save his country in the name of the Lord. Since he was from a poor family and least in his father's house Gideon asked the angel to show him a sign that he had talked to the angel. He was given the sign, but later we see him asking God for another sign so he would know he was supposed to lead an army of men against the enemy.

When we hear a person say, "I put a fleece before the Lord", they are going back to the story of Gideon. He took the lambs wool (fleece) and asked God to show him he was supposed to obey by making the wool dry when all around was wet with dew, and even asked God a second time to show him by making the fleece wet and all around it dry. God shows the humanity of these people by letting us know their weakness of faith when He asked them to do something.

Read: Judges 7:19-22

Caring for others, speaking the truth and living with integrity are not always rewarded in this broken world. We wonder why everyone does not love and respect us when we are doing our best to live a Christian life each day. Let's look at Paul this morning. As long as he was persecuting Christians, he was very popular with the religious and political people. But, when he began a different life, he exposed the pharisees, priests, and others who were putting on a show of living for God, but it was only outward. When the real person was brought to light, they resented it, and even became hostile toward Paul. They enlisted a skilled orator, Tertullus, who flattered the governor and represented them in their case against Paul.

We encounter some of this treatment, today, as people call Christians names and in some countries there those who are killed for becoming Christian. There are unbelievers who want to take all thoughts of Christ from the people. This includes memorial signs and even the word Christmas. Some want the ten commandments, which have been displayed for many years, taken away. Even though it is not popular to stand as a Christian, let us pray that God will give us the strength to stand against the wiles of Satan.

Read: Ephesians 6:10-13

*E*ven though a person has accepted Jesus as Savior, he or she may let Satan tempt them and when they dwell on this temptation and finally give in to it, they not only have the chance of ruining their lives, but each person has to answer to the results of that sin. Sure, God will forgive, but there is payment due. For instance, Rebekah lied to her husband about her sons. She helped Jacob deceive him and steal the blessing due the oldest son. How was she punished for her sin? Her favorite son, Jacob, ran away to keep Esau from killing him because of his deception. We never find the mother, Rebekah, seeing her son again.

We, as Christians, are able to trust God and live a great life, or get away from him and suffer the consequences. What is the solution, then, when we have wandered away? Turn back to God, asking Him to forgive you, making everything right with your fellowman, and determining to live a life as close to the Lord as possible.

Read: Gen. 27:41-43

God wants to bless His children, but it is important for each of us to trust Him and expect Him to do what is best for us. When the twelve men were sent to spy out the land of Canaan, the land God had promised them, they found a great land that was rich in fruit and called it a land of milk and honey. But there was something that made them fearful and that was the people who lived there. They were great strong men. They saw walled cities and the mountains and went back to Moses and the people saying, "we can't." This was the account of the majority and that was ten spies who were afraid and decided they could not take the the land God had given them. There were two, which was a minority as Christians are today, who said , "yes we can." Caleb and Joshua said, "Let us go up at once and possess the land God has given us."

Reading this, you will see the congregation lost faith in their leader and forgot the mighty power of God. For their unbelief and distrust in God, they wandered in the wilderness for forty years until all the older generation was gone. Are Christians looking around today at all the political ploys and anti-christian propaganda and saying, "We are a minority, we can't fight all this." You are right, but God can. We must trust Him and submit to His will for us.

Read: Numbers 14:27-29

I read something in "Touched by an E-mail and I think it is a great deal of "food for thought." What if God took away the Bible tomorrow because we failed to read it today? How important is God's Word to you and me? It is the Lamp unto our feet and It will light our path from day to day. But in order to have God's Word light our path and guide us, we must study it, asking God to open our minds with the understanding to know what He is telling us. When we stand before God, ignorance will be no excuse for those of us who have dozens of Bibles at our finger tips all the time. From where do we obtain knowledge?

In the Book of Hosea God said, "My people are destroyed because of their lack of knowledge." If we do not study our Bibles, we will not know what God is saying to us. God has granted us the wonderful blessing of living in a country that is free. This freedom should not be taken for granted, and it is ours for which to stand. When a child in school cannot say "Bless you" when someone sneezes in school we need to take notice that our freedom is gradually being taken away. There is a famine in the land, that is a famine of listening, learning, respecting and living by God's Word. Do you tell your child stories from the Bible or do you tell them ghostly stories?

Read: Hosea 4:6

Yesterday we talked about reading the Bible because It is the Lamp of God to guide us in this life. When we get into God's Word, we do not have excuses for not serving Him. Everything we face in life is answered in His Word. We might have a task we do not know how to handle and we say, "it is impossible," but God's Word says, "all things are possible." With His help you can do all things (Philippians 4:13) but you say, "I am not able to face this and survive," "I just cannot manage this" God's Word tells us He is able and He will supply all our needs.

Now we have these answers, we are still unsure and we say, "With all these troubles, I am so worried and frustrated" and God tells us in (First Peter 5: 6 & 7) to cast our cares (troubles) on Him. Satan then tells us, "God is not hearing you, and you are all alone in your troubles." Not true, the child of God is never alone.

Read: Hebrews 13:5

One of the greatest tools Satan has to use against a Christian is fear. You might say, "I am not afraid." Do you worry about the sorrows tomorrow might bring? That is a kind of fear. The things we fear the most are usually things that never happen. It is only a ploy of Satan to keep us from trusting God, for putting all our life into His Hands and leaving it there. We know God is all powerful and we pray to Him daily asking Him for the things we need.

Are we afraid God will not hear our prayer, or He will answer "no" when we are earnestly asking Him for something? When we are afraid it shows a lack of faith in our Heavenly Father. Some facts we should remember are these: If we belong to God, He is our Father and He says in the scripture He will not give His child a stone when he ask for bread (Matt. 7: 9). He promises to be with His children. We have nothing to be afraid of because the Comforter is with us in this life and when we are dying, like Stephen, a Christian can say, "I see Jesus standing" He will be waiting for you.

Read: Matthew 28:20

$\mathcal{D}$o you want to be a Christian that is a survivor or do you want to give up and sit in a dark corner crying "woe is me?" The happy person does not dwell on fears and frustrations, but hopes and dreams. Are you thinking about the time you tried and failed or what is still possible for you to accomplish? Do you want to be a survivor?

Maybe you have had pain and sorrow, but God never promised us a life free of pain and sorrow, but His precious promise is "I will be with you". The words of an old Hymn, I remember are these: "He will give me peace and glory and go with me all the way." In other words, God has sent the Holy Spirit to comfort and guide His children all through this life. If you belong to the Heavenly Father, His Love will enfold you just like a blanket wrapped around you. When we have troubled times let us think of Him this way and cry out to Him to let His presence be known and give us the strength we need.

Read: Deuteronomy 31:6

September

When we read the prophecies in Jeremiah, we see God directing him to go to different places and giving him messages there for his people. The people had gotten away from the Lord and Jeremiah wept for them and preached to them but they refused to listen. One of the most beautiful lessons is the Potter's House lesson. God told him to go down to the potter's house and he watched the potter as he worked. We can clearly see this scene. The potter puts a lump of clay on the wheel and turns it to make a beautiful vessel, but the vessel was flawed.

This is the life of each Christian. Even though we have access to Jesus and can pray in His name we can get away from God and forget His wonderful love for us. But, just like the vessel, God is the Master Potter and He will mold and make us again into a vessel He can use. Remember, David prayed to God, "Restore again to me the joy of Thy salvation." The people had gotten away from God and Jeremiah's message was "turn again to God." Our nation needs this message, we must pray that people will see it.

Read: Psalm 139:1-6

When we look at the parable of the mustard seed, we think of our mustard growing in a patch of greens. It gets only about five or six inches tall, at the most. When I was in the Holy Land, I had a chance to see a mustard plant. The mustard plant there is totally different from the mustard plant we grow. Jesus was giving a beautiful, meaningful parable, as always. The mustard plant I saw was taller than I am, and the seeds we gathered from it were smaller than our mustard seed. They are in a pod and very small. Remembering these seed we realize our faith is small, but Jesus also gave the mustard seed in comparing the Kingdom of God.

We do not usually notice this parable. When the Word of God is sown it becomes great in this earth. God said, "My Word will not return void". From a small beginning we see God's Word flourish. From the beginning the few told about Jesus, but now His Name is known to millions. "Little is much when God is in it."

Read: Mark 4:30-32

*H*ow careful are we with our words? There is a story about a parent teaching a child to hold his temper. The child was to drive a nail into wood each time he lost his temper and the nails became fewer, because the child was thinking about what he was saying and learning to hold his anger. Finally, with the lesson learned, the parent told him he would have to pull the nails out. Seeing the holes he left in the wood was a real lesson to the youth. When we say things in anger, they hurt others, things will never be the same between you and the person you have hurt. You might say, "I'm sorry," but the nail has been driven in and a hole is left in the heart of the person you have hurt.

We should pray that God will give us the wisdom to build others up, instead of tearing them down with angry words. A verbal wound is as hurtful as a physical one. Our tongue can be a terrible weapon. We need to ask God to help us control our speech.

Read: James 3:8-11

God wants us to communicate with Him. How much do we pray each day? The Scriptures tell us to "pray without ceasing." This does not mean we are to stay on our knees all day, but we can go in an attitude of prayer. God wants us to cry out to Him when we have a time of crisis, and He wants us to us to ask Him for peace of mind when we need comfort.

Let us not forget to thank Him for His goodness and praise Him for who He is and what He has done for each of us. We should come to God with everything we are and everything we have. He is never to busy to listen to His child and He is waiting. Call to Him, sing to Him, cry to Him because it doesn't matter He cares for you.

Read: Micah 7:7 and Psalm 145:1-3

*H*umble people never need to talk about how humble they are or how much they serve the Lord. The reason there is no need to talk about what your service is this: Actions speak louder than words. How many people do we see today who "talk the talk" but do not "walk the walk". This is hypocrisy and the lives Jesus condemned in the Pharisees over and over. Why can we not see and know that God sees through a veil of pretense? Pretending to be Christian might fool a number of people but God knows us through and through. He knows our thoughts and we do nothing in secret.

Let us live for Jesus sincerely and realize we do not need to draw attention to ourselves. We live for Jesus because we love Him and we "walk the walk" each day because we know it pleases the one who has hung on a cross, suffered and died so that we each could gain eternal life. Our lives should back up our talk.

Read: Matthew 6:1-5

What do you teach your children and grandchildren and others who look to you for guidance? In the Book of Genesis we see a mother teaching her son to deceive his father. The very name Jacob meant deceiver, but he had a choice and that choice was to honor his father. I see a family with jealousy and no love one for another when I look at this story. Even though the father had become blind, he had shown earlier in life he loved one son more than the other. The mother loved Jacob and the father loved Esau. More than that, when the father was getting ready to die we see no compassion from the mother, but we see her conniving to fool him, who could not see and helping he favorite steal the blessing from his brother. I think Jacob was converted later when we find him wrestling with the angel.

We, as Christians, see how wrong these parents were, but we also know that we pay for our sins, even on earth, the results of our actions are there before us. When we study this Scripture, I never find a place that tells me Rebekah saw her favorite son again before she died, because she had to send him away to keep Esau from killing him.

Read: Gen. 27:6-13

*A*re you bitter, holding grudges against someone? There is something a Christian should always remember. Bitterness and unforgiveness doesn't hurt the unforgiven, but the one holding these grudges. When we read the book "Hiding Place" by Corrie Ten Boon and see how the Nazis captured her and her family, imprisoned them and tortured them we see how much the human being has to endure in the face of evil. After the war Corrie cared for others who had been treated as she had and lived. She had lost all the rest of her family and was filled with hate toward the ones who had done these deeds. She discovered that only the ones who could forgive were the truly free ones.

When we carry a load of bitterness inside us, we cannot get through to God even though we cry out to Him. This hatred will be a wall between us and Him. When we forgive as He has forgiven us, we are free. It takes God's strength to help us forgive, but with His help we can do so and we will not be stuck in bitterness, anymore. When we hear Jesus say, "Father forgive them" we know what we should do.

Read: Matthew 6:12-15

*I*n your mind, what do you see when you hear the word surrender? Do you see pictures of soldiers returning from battle, bloody, wounded and defeated? We see that as a negative word, but when we say surrender to Jesus Christ it means a totally different thing. When we surrender to Him, we have defeated all the thoughts Satan has flung at us and we win. When a person surrenders his or her life to Jesus there is no hanging of the head in defeat, but hands raised in victory.

One person writes that we each must surrender daily. The meaning of this is we ask God each morning to take over our life. We ask Him to give us the victory over each thought that isn't right, help us use the language that will be a testimony to others, and show us kindnesses we need to perform as we go about our daily routine. We ask Him to help us forgive others as He has forgiven us. Have you asked God to take over your life today? Have you surrendered your will to Him?

Read: Psalm 25:4 & 5

*H*ave you heard a person or people make the statement of a person like this: He or she is not religious enough or they are too religious? Did you ever think that people would say, even though Christ left Heaven and came to us, He was not religious enough? This was the chief complaint against Him by the Pharisees and all the religious leaders of the day. Even though Jesus walked on water, healed the blind and did miracles that had never been done before, the religious leaders came after Him because they said He didn't keep the Sabbath, and their man made laws. In other words, He did not fit the mold. Religion can be the belief in anything, whether it is of God or not.

Jesus came to earth to accomplish what God had for Him to do, and He did that when He died on the cross so we could be forgiven for our sins. The conclusion we need to come to is this: It is not putting on a big show, showing how religious we are, but living a Christian life, doing what God created us to do. Asking Him and following His will. That's all God asks of us.

Read: John 17:1-4

We are not to think more of ourselves than we ought. God had Saul anointed King when he was little in his own sight. (1st Samuel 15:17) We could say he knew he was nothing without God and so it is with each of us. This is the time God made Him head of the tribes of Israel. When we read about him and others, we find that power made them forget God. When Saul was told to destroy all the enemy, he saved some, which displeased God, and caused him grief. When a person, in power, is confronted with their sin they are quick to blame someone else as Saul did. He told Samuel, the prophet, he did what God had said, but the people saved the spoil and he even made the excuse the people kept the spoil to sacrifice to the Lord.

The entire lesson here is this: We might sacrifice our time, money, and do all the works we can think of and God wants obedience, first. When we do not obey Him all the other things are as nothing in His sight. Our society has become one of excuses. Because of this or that, I have acted or this person or that one caused me to do the wrong things. No matter the excuses we make, we will each stand before a Holy God one day, responsible for ourselves.

Read: 1st Samuel 15:22 & 23

*W*hen we were children and had no phones to play with, we would have competitive games. Each person tried to make the other one "give up." In the "grown-up" world there will be troubles and sorrows, but we are never to "give up." Becoming a person who never gives up might cost us, because progress has a price. We might say, "I want to walk closer to Jesus, I want to grow spiritually". Are you willing to pay the price? What could these costs be? We might lose a friend, set aside some habits we know God is not pleased with, and even risk annoying family members, or lose a few minutes of sleep.

If you have not read "The Pilgrim's Progress," this book illustrates how our journey to the Celestial City will take us through all manner of sloughs and valleys. So it is with the Christian life. Jesus has promised He will be with us in all the troubles we have and we are never to give up. We are to pray for a closer walk with Him. The final reward is OUT OF THIS WORLD, IT IS HEAVEN!

Read: Matthew 16:24-26

*H*ow do we respond to different circumstances during the day? When there is no milk left for cereal, when we get in a traffic jam, someone slights us and would not speak, or we go to the store to get the needed milk and there is a long line. What if we stopped and praised God for each of these circumstances? The traffic jam might have kept us from an accident down the road and God could have meant for us to talk to someone in that long line at the grocery store. How about the one who would not speak to me? Maybe God wanted you to react as a Christian should, smile, speak and go on your way, thus showing the right attitude.

We need to ask God to help us through each day, showing us the right way to handle anything that happens to us. We need to praise Him for who is and the Scripture tells us to pray without ceasing. If we are in a prayerful mood when these things happen to us we will be able to thank God that we are here, even though things aren't perfect in our lives. When we truly worship God there is no room for anger or self-pity. Think on His Goodness, His majesty!

Read: Psalm 71:14-17

*I*f you belong to Jesus, God is your father and when we have God as our Father we never have to fear. We see David, a young lad going against the giant. He did not need armor, but used only a sling. He knew God would direct the stone. He believed in the power of God. We see Gideon threshing wheat and the angel calling him a mighty man of valour. He was a poor person, according to the world's riches, but God told him to go and promised to be with him. We see God taking down so many of the warriors he had, and then we see the miracle of the wall falling. A wall or a giant is nothing to God.

Sometimes we see a wall or a giant in front of us and we think we cannot survive, but we as Christians must remember that God is with us in all our hardships which we could call giants or walls. We think of Peter and the other apostles in prison for preaching Jesus and the angel opening prison doors. The tomb could not hold Lazarus, and we see many more miracles done by God to those who prayed and believed. Remember faith and prayer will remove the mountains in our lives. Believe this: As long as God has work for us to do on this earth He will take care of every situation, and when our work is finished, He will take us home to be with Him in Heaven.

Read: Acts 12:5-11

Do we always want things to go our way? "No, not that way, let me show you how I want it done." We pray for God to walk with us, daily, to show us His will and what He wants us to do for Him. When He steps in to change our lives we say, "Not that way, Lord." This is rebellion against the very things we pray for. We do not say these words aloud, but we are guilty of thinking that way, many times. We want to direct God's actions. God promises He will work His best for us, but we assume His best for us matches what we think is best for us.

If we really want God's will and God's best in our lives we need to trust Him enough to let Him do it His way. We do not know the future and we do not always know what will be best for us, but God is in control. Even though we make decisions on our own, He comes to our rescue when things go wrong. He takes bad things and works them for a way to serve Him, or we might say He works them out for good.

Read: Psalm 77:11-13

Did you know there is more than one way to rebel against God? There is the kind of rebellion that kicks up it's heels at the authority of God and His Word. But there is another kind of rebellion we need to think about and that is hiding from the God. There are many ways we might hide from His Will. We can hide in busyness and in overcommitment. That is,we can hide by doing many good things convincing ourselves we are in God's will, but these may not be God's things. When we go on our own, making decisions without praying about them, we are saying to God we do not want or need to hear from Him. Why would we have this attitude? Because God might make us change our plans or our direction. He might make us stop, and listen to Him.

The truth is this: We cannot hide from God and when we try with all our own busyness we are missing out on the outrageously love of God. His Love is what we need to fill our hearts with joy. We have a song from long ago and the words are this: "Hear Him calling out your name, reach out you can touch Him, you will never be the same." Come into the light and ask God's will for your life.

Read: Psalm 40:1-3

When we pray do we remember to ask God to give us wisdom to understand His Word? I am sure this has always been true, but we should be aware we live in a time we need to understand the messages of the Bible. Do you read something and as we have heard many say "it is as clear as mud?" If this happens to you, read it again and again if necessary. Ask God to help you understand. The person who is wise will study to show himself or herself approved, rightly dividing the Word of Truth and asking God to show you His will from His Word. There are ways to worship God during the day we might not have thought of.

We can speak to ourselves with psalms, hymns, and spiritual songs and that is making melody in our hearts. We can keep a prayer of thanksgiving in our hearts during the day as we go about our daily tasks. How thankful are we that Jesus was willing to suffer a horrible death on the cross for us? We need to wake up and realize we, as Christians, are to be the light of the world. Let us make use of our time on earth.

Read: Ephesians 5:14-17

Do we really trust God enough to say, "whatever comes, I know God will give me the strength to deal with it". In this life we have many unexpected things to happen to us. We might get up to a bright day with sunshine and have storms before night. God knows what we are going to face, and it is very good He does not let us see the future. In our future we might have many twists, turns of life, betrayal, job loss, and physical or financial troubles. God has promised us we will not go through whatever comes our way alone.

Remember He is always there to wipe away our tears, hold us tight and calm out fears. Let us each give "whatever" to God because when we put it into His Hands, He will hold us up, walk with us, listen to us, give us the courage we need each day and finally take us home to be with Him in the beautiful place He has gone to prepare for each person who will accept Him as Savior and Lord.

Read: Psalm 23

God is the amazing Creator. Let us get a small vision of His creation. He made everyone different from the next person. He could have made us all exactly alike, but He chose to build a variety into humanity. Our differences can be eye color, hair color, skin color, but the one thing we have in common is that God created us all. Also Jesus came to earth, suffered and died for each person. When we look at a person, do we look critically or do we see the soul God created and the one Jesus died for? There are no favorites with God. In the Old Testament we find He chose the Jewish Nation, through Abraham, and promised to be their God if they would trust Him.

Now, when we accept Jesus Christ, we become one of His children and He is our God, also. He wants each of us to reach out to others in love and understanding, to teach, live in peace without prejudice and hatred. We need to follow the example Jesus gave us, and that is love and forgiveness. You might say, "but see what that person did to me," and the answer is this, "vengeance is mine, saith the Lord, I will repay."

Read: Romans 12:19-21

*T*his morning we think of the song, "Savior, like a shepherd lead us" and we then think of the following words, "much we need Thy tender care." When the shepherd calls his sheep each morning, he is ready to gather them together and as he sets off for the day's journey the sheep follow him. The sheep watch the shepherd, because they know they can trust him to give them green grass to eat. They also know he will carry them to still waters to drink. Notice he does not carry them to swift flowing waters that can carry them away, but to a place of peace and stillness.

When Jesus is our Shepherd, we know He will not take us on paths too steep or risky and when we get into briars, thistles or fall into a ditch, He will pick us up. The day is gone, or we should say the years of our lives are spent following Him, and now it is time for Him to take His sheep safely home. Jesus bought us with His precious blood, and we should trust Him, never looking back.

Read: Isaiah 40:10 & 11

*H*ow thankful are we for the blessings we receive each day? Years ago when we were in Israel our guide told us Americans were the most spoiled people in the world because they complained about the food. Do we take everything we have each day for granted? Do we sit at a table laden with food and neglect to thank God for it? We find in the Book of Luke there were ten lepers, who went to Jesus for help. A leper would have been put away from other people and was considered to have one of the most dreaded diseases. Even today we have missionaries who work with the lepers who have to stay in colonies, because of spreading the sickness that kills. Were the ten lepers thankful they had been healed of this awful thing? When we look into the story we find only one, a Samaritan, came back to thank Jesus and glorify God.

Let us remember our very breath is given us by God. Stop! Thank Jesus for coming to this earth from Heaven and suffering, dying on a cross so we can be saved. Thank Him for sending the Comforter, the Holy Spirit, to guide and teach us. Thank Him for His promise that He will return for each of us and carry us to be with Him in Heaven.

Read: Luke 17:12-17

*A*re we guilty of denying Jesus Christ? Our first answer will be "of course not", but what about the opportunity you missed when you were talking to someone who did not know Him? What are the excuses we use? We have heard these excuses many times. They could be:

1. People keep religion private and do not discuss it with others.
2. If I say something that isn't politically correct, people will think I am ignorant.
3. I might make person feel bad and they will not want to stay around me anymore.

These are just some of the ways we might find ourselves denying Christ.

We know we are not to back people into a corner, because there is a right way of telling about Jesus. We can always tell the things Jesus has done for us, letting our light shine so others will see our faith in Him. No, we do not do the same way Peter did by saying , "I never knew Him," but we must realize we are the only Bible some people will read and walk each day so that people will know we belong to Jesus.

Read: John 18:25 & 26

*W*e hear the question, "what time is it?" The time asked is what hour of the day is it, but God has told us to redeem the time and this means we are to use the time we have on earth worshiping and serving, and trusting in Him.

We look at David this morning. He was a man after God's own heart and he was a good king for a time. He depended on and followed God's instructions. In looking at his life we see him getting away from God with the counting of Israel. In other words, he allowed Satan to get him to do something that was displeasing to God. This year is almost gone and there is a question we should ask ourselves. "Am I as close to God as I was this time a year ago?" "Have I allowed other things to come between God and me?" Satan gradually gets us away from God by putting other things and yes, other people in our path sometimes. David got away from God and finally did not go out to battle, anymore. He put himself into the position to be tempted by watching Bathsheba. Had he been in service of the Lord, in battle, Satan would not have had this opportunity to tempt him.

Let us, each, take inventory today and earnestly search our hearts, asking God to draw us nearer to Him.

Read: Psalm 51:9-12

*H*ow consistent are we in making time for the Lord each day? It does not matter if you meet with Him morning or evening, but it does matter that we are there regularly. Our Father, God, wants to meet with us, listen to us, talk to us and have a time of quiet communion each day. God speaks to us through His Word, which we should study to show ourselves approved and then He waits for us to talk or pray to Him.

There are many things that may keep us from stopping long enough to talk to Him. We might have someone sick at night and lose sleep, get up late and have to hurry to work and there could be a dozen other reasons we neglect talking to God. He is there all the time and our time with Him is precious. When you take time to really commune with God, you will gain joy, come away refreshed and have a much better day or night. This is a need we all have, daily.

Read: Luke 10:38-42

*I*n the Book of 2nd Chronicles we find Solomon praying for God to listen to his plea. He asked God to remember the mercies He had promised David and the prayer was such that when he finished fire came down from heaven and glory filled the house of God. The fire had consumed the sacrifices on the altar and the people knew that God was there. They bowed down to worship Him and their statement was "He is good , for His mercy endureth forever." After such a wonderful experience the people went away glad because the goodness of the Lord had been shown to them.

In the verses of Chapter 7, God is telling Solomon he has heard his prayer and He is also letting the king know He is all powerful, in verses 12 &13. God has shown America His goodness again and again, and we need to bow our faces to the ground and beg Him to forgive and restore favor to our country. He made a promise to these people and that promise still holds today.

Read: 2nd Chronicles 7:14.

We know we cannot understand another person until we have walked a mile in their shoes. To understand how Jesus lived and served we need to slide our feet into His sandals. He told us He came not to be served but to serve, thus showing us the route to happiness. This is the meaning of, "It is more blessed to give than to receive." Do we love others with a servant love? If we have the kind of love Jesus has for us we will be patient and compassionate. We will love others outside our circle of friends and favorite people.

How do you feel when you have done a service for someone and that person did not thank you or even recognize the help you gave him or her? It is very hard to love and pray for him or her, but Jesus is our example. Jesus helped many with no thanks and only beating and the cross as His reward on earth. He prayed for those who persecuted Him and killed Him. Jesus is our only way to happiness. We should try on His sandals and we will find they will fit perfectly.

Read: 1st Peter 2:21

"*I*s there any Word from the Lord?" This is the question we hear Jeremiah being asked when Zedekiah, the king knew he was in great trouble. The answer Jeremiah gave him was not good, because God had said Zedekiah's kingdom would be delivered into the hands of Babylon. There was another Word from God and that Word was the prediction of Jesus coming to earth to save the lost. "And the Word became flesh and dwelt among us." John 1:14 Jesus also said "I will rise after the third day," and He did. He told His disciples to stay in Jerusalem and the Comforter would come endowing them with power from on high. When God gives us a Word or we might say Message it will come true and today we have a Word from Him. Yes, we might ask "is there a Word from the Lord for us?"

Jesus left this message with us, "Take heed that ye be not deceived, for many shall come in my name, do not follow them. While the disciples stood gazing into the heavens when Jesus ascended the angel came and gave them the promise we are looking forward to each day.

Read: Acts 1:11 This is the Word from the Lord.

*T*here are those who do not believe in life after death and others who say we are not to think of those things. The idea is we are to live our lives as we will, one day at a time until the end. These, of course, are wrong ideas about life. Each of us has a beginning of time and each of us will have an end. The most important decision any one of us will make between the beginning and the end is this: Ask Jesus to forgive our sin, trust Him and live for Him. Think on this, "This is life eternal, that they may know Thee, the only true God whom thou hast sent." (John 17:3) We are not to morn our loved ones as though we will never see them again, but remember the promise of Jesus when He said, "I go to prepare a place for you and I will come again and receive you unto myself that where I am there you may be also."

The real greatness of life is not in the few years we live on earth, but rather that we are to live forever with Jesus Christ who loved us so much He came to earth to prepare a way for us to have eternal life. If you are discouraged, take hope, God is on the throne and He sees all the troubles you have and if you will trust Him, completely, He will carry your burdens on earth and when the end of your life comes, He will take you home to heaven.

Read: 1st Thessalonians 4:13-17

We sing, "Oh the Blood of Jesus, it washes white as snow," but do we really realize the importance of the precious blood shed for us. There was a pastor called to pray for a boy in a very poor neighborhood and the father made the remark, "the doctor said if he had a blood transfusion, he would have a chance to live." The Pastor saw that the money was contributed so the boy could have the transfusion and when he saw the boy later, he was well and received Christ as his savior and Lord. This is what Jesus did for us. He looked down and saw a dying world, a world that was all wrong and He cared enough to leave heaven and live among the people on earth, receiving terrible treatment, die on the cross, and shed His blood so we could have a blood transfusion or we say, be saved.

Today, we see the world is all wrong, but do we care? Most serious of all is our attitude of indifference. He calls and we do not respond, He knocks and we do not hear. Measured by Calvary, how do we look? To refuse Jesus and what He offered us on the cross is to perish, to accept Him is to live.

Read: Luke 23:33 & 34

❦ *September 29* ❦

We hear people mention "the Gospel" and someone might wonder at this statement. What is the Gospel? Sometimes a person might define it as the death, burial and resurrection of our Lord. I would say the Gospel is the entire story. The virgin Birth of Jesus, His death for our sin, His burial and His resurrection. I cannot leave out the message He left with us when He said, "I go to prepare a place for you and I will come again and receive you unto myself, that where I am, there ye may be also." When we look at this we see the story of Jesus. He was beaten and wounded for our sins or transgressions, bruised for our iniquities and by His stripes we are healed. Paul said, "God forbid that I should glory save in the cross of our Lord Jesus Christ." The Christian church from the time of the apostles has had one theme and that is Christ and Him crucified. Let us think of Christ in this way:

If you or I had been the only living soul He would have suffered and died for anyone of us. He came to seek and to save every person who would accept Him. He is no respecter of persons. The world was dark, because Satan had people in bondage or we could say slavery of sin. We needed a perfect sacrifice to go to God, shed His blood and give us a choice. "Hallelujah! what a Saviour!"

Read: Isaiah 53:3-6

*L*et us think of the first step of coming to Jesus, today. The Bible says as Moses lifted up the serpent in the wilderness even so must the Son of man be lifted up; that whosoever believeth in Him should not parish, but have everlasting life. The first step is repentance. The word means being sorry for our sin and believing God will save us, so we ask him to forgive us and save us.

When we are sincere, asking for forgiveness and willing to turn from the unbelieving way we have been living and turn to Jesus Christ, we will be forgiven and on our way to the place Jesus went away to prepare for us. This place is called Heaven. We must remember God does the work of saving each person, and we call that "washing in the blood" because Jesus shed His blood so that we could each be saved. So, the answers here are simple. We come to Jesus, asking forgiveness and believing He will save us as He said He would, and the redemption part is taken care of by God through Jesus Christ. Redemption is another word we need to remember.

When we are unsaved we are slaves to sin and when a person is bought out of slavery it is called redeeming. This is what Jesus did for us on the Cross!

Read: John 3:16-18

October

God created a beautiful world for man to enjoy. When we think of the garden of Eden, we realize it must have been more beautiful than we can imagine. The question is this: "What happened to the beautiful world God created?" Satan came on the scene in the Book of Genesis and enticed the woman and man to listen to him, and we see the downfall of humanity. God moved the beautiful garden and forced man to begin earning his bread by the sweat of his face and the woman was to bear the children. Since that time, we see the evils Satan brings about in the human life. We see greed, murder, debauchery of all kind and the tearing down of the natural beauty God created.

We must wonder what God sees when He looks down upon the world He created. He knew mankind needed a remedy for sin and Jesus came to earth to live, die and rise again to give man a chance to live in a beautiful place after this life. I have been asked the question, "what happened to the tree of life?" The answer is: It is on either side of the river of life in Heaven. Rev. 22:2 The fall season is upon us and we will see the beautiful colors of autumn. The gold, orange and brown of the leaves. Stop, and enjoy the beauty that is still with us, created by God.

Read: 1st Timothy 6:17

I read an article that went like this: "The older I get the closer I become to God." We might have gray hair, wrinkles and age spots, but what about all that is on the inside? These things mentioned above, we try to control with creams, gels and hair color, but we must realize the outside of our bodies does not define the beauty of "us" inside. As age comes on we need to be like snowballs when they roll along.

We gather experience, skills, friends, connections, wisdom and should be gathering spiritual wisdom on God's Word. Of course this wisdom comes only from God and when we seek it, He will give it to us. Knowledge is the things we read and see in books, but wisdom is the inner understanding God gives us. Also, after we gain these things from life we are willing to share them with others who are younger and those in need. Thank God for allowing us to grow older. We are to accept this as a gift to share with others.

Read: Proverbs 21:2 & 21

*P*eople are talking about making bucket lists and when asked why are you making a bucket list, the answer is this: "These are the things I want or the things I want to do before I die." Does this tell us that most people are not satisfied with the pleasures and treasures they have. When a person makes a "bucket" list they might be able to go some of these places or get some of these things, but are these things that will bring satisfaction and peace? In fact if each goal was met would it bring peace to the person seeking it? There is no guarantee that anything on your list will bring you the pleasure and satisfaction you desire, or is there one thing that has been left out?

There is a map to this treasure and that is God's Word. This map is waiting to be discovered and it is not hidden from view. Everyone can share it. What is the treasure? God, Himself, is the treasure and He is yours for the asking. He is the one true companion that will bring peace.

Read: Matthew 7:7 & 8

*W*e want to keep our bodies healthy so we take vitamins each day, and eat the things that are good for us, knowing we have one body and if we wish to be of service to God and others we must keep it as strong as we can. When we look into God's Word we will see that It gives us the recipe for a healthy spirit or we might say soul. We know God is the Great Physician who invests in a healthy soul. What is the prescriptions He gives for a healthy, vibrant spiritual life? They are faith, prayer and study in God's Word, daily. These are the vitamins of the soul. When we have faith, worry will flee, and we will know that God takes care of future circumstances we cannot see. We will trust Him to take care of these things. As we study His Word and pray we will be strengthened in our connection with Him.

Let us always remember we are responsible for watching over our bodies, but God is the Great Physician who watches over our souls. In Luke Chapter 11, we find the prayer that is called the Lord's Prayer, but it is a model prayer. He is teaching us how to pray.

Read: 2nd Timothy 2:15

$\mathcal{A}$ sincere humble Christian does not have to go around bragging about how good they are or what they are doing for God, because this shows in their actions from day to day. In each interaction a Christian has, his or her faith will shine through. The dealings will be honest, sincere and caring. Does it not make us cringe to hear a person "talk the talk" and not "walk the walk?" The acts put on for people are for a show, but God sees the real person. He looks on the heart or we should say the inner person. He knows our thoughts and sees each action. Some of Jesus' most biting remarks had to do with the way of the Pharisees. He easily saw through the veil of hypocrisy and He cautioned His followers to avoid such behavior. We say we want to live for Jesus, then let us live for Him daily.

We do not need to blow a trumpet or shout about our lives because our actions are the testimony other people see. Would you listen to a person talk about Jesus when you see the same person next week talking and walking against God's Word? We are to "walk the walk" because we love Him and God who sees in secret will be pleased with us.

Read: Matthew 6:2 & 16-18

*T*his morning let us think of the ultimate character of God. His character is immeasurable love, profound patience, infinite mercy and eternal righteousness.

God's purpose is the salvation of all men. He said, "why will ye die, O house of Israel? For I have no pleasure in the death of him that dieth saith the Lord God." He is talking about spiritual death not physical death. Because of Adam and Eve we are all born in sin with a barrier between us and God. The only way the barrier can be removed is through repentance and faith. All people will not be saved, even though God would have it so. This is a personal choice, but there are those who would stay in a depraved, vile life and refuse to ask God to forgive them. No matter the life a person has had before, God is waiting for him or her to come in repentance (sorry for the sins committed) and cry out to Him for forgiveness. The capacity for faith is born in us, but many go through long years of defiance and evil living and saying "no" to God and become so hard, they do not know God is speaking to them, anymore. God sends no person to Hell. Each individual has a choice in this life. We are free to choose God or Satan. If a person falls into a gutter, drunken, drugged, with vile language coming from his or her lips, this is a choice they have made for their life.

Read: John 3:16-20

*T*here are times when we feel that we are not as close to God as we were at one time. At a time like this we need to search ourselves and ask, "Have I let the cares of this world come into my life in such a way, that I have not studied and prayed as I should have?" "Have I let worry over a loved one take over my thoughts instead of giving that worry to God?" "Have I allowed myself to give in to the temptation of putting other things before going to worship?" All these things are used by Satan to get us away from God. He will give us excuses and yes, we will even call them reasons not to worship God first. We can gradually get away from the joy He has given us in the past. Remember David said, Lord restore unto me the joy of Thy salvation.

God gave Jeremiah the message of the potter's house. He wanted the nation (and of course this goes for individuals) to know he was the creator and He could remold and remake them into the vessel He wanted them to be. Isn't it time to ask God to remold us because we have become marred and gotten away from Him? He cannot used a marred vessel, but waits for us to come to Him for a renewing and He will make us usable for Himself, and restore the joy of His salvation

Read: Jeremiah 18:3-6

*W*e find in Proverbs from the wisdom of Solomon, the way to look unto the Lord. In Chapter 2, verse 2 of Proverbs the writer is advising a young person to listen to the knowledge that is taught him or her and to apply it. Of course, these young ones could be those we call the "babes" in Christ. They are those who are converted or we would say have come to Jesus, but have never grown because they had no mentor, no person to take an interest in them, befriend them, teach them and lead them to become more mature Christians. I know it is the responsibility of a new Christian to study as Paul told Timothy, but what if they have not been taught the need of study and prayer or we might say the need to gain the knowledge and wisdom found in God's Word? What if they have not thought of God speaking to us through His Word and the joy we have of talking to Him in prayer?

Do we search for the understanding of God's Word as we would search for silver or gold? It is much more precious, because the riches of this world will pass away, but God's Word remains true. Every Word of God is Pure and is a shield or buckler keeping us secure.

Read: Proverbs 4:5-7

Do you feel alone and as if all your loved ones have forsaken you today? We live in a day of people staying so busy they do not take time to say "I love you", and this should not be. As we go about our daily routine do we realize there are people who live alone, people who need just a smile or a hug to let them know you care. When Jesus walked on this earth He showed love to all people. There were lepers, crippled ones, those sick for many years, and He healed them all treating them the same, showing He cared. If you feel alone, I would say having a "pity party" today, look around you. There are many less fortunate and if you know Jesus Christ, you are most wealthy, and you have a friend that sticketh closer than a brother, because He walks with you and He is with you all the time. He loves each of us the same and He gives us a choice to accept Him as our personal Savior and Lord. If you do not know Him, you are missing His fellowship and also the assurance of everlasting life in Heaven.

If you are feeling "down" today, look to Jesus, asking Him to lift you up and show you someone who needs your encouragement, then, if you belong to Him, get busy about the Father's business.

Read: Luke 2:41-43 & 46-49

We should stop today and realize what Jesus did for each of us. He has no favorites, but He died for every soul. We find the prophecy of His treatment by the human race in Isaiah. We should stop and realize this was written hundreds of years before Jesus was born, but God gave the prophecy to the people and it all came true. Isaiah Chapter 53 tells us the story of the suffering Savior. All we like sheep have gone astray, or we would say we are all sinful human beings and each human being wants to go his own way. Because of this, Jesus was led as a lamb to the slaughter. He went willingly and opened not His mouth. He was beaten so much He could not be recognized and yet He was willing to hang on a cross and die so that each of us could be saved.

The Scripture even tells us where He was going to be buried. He was buried in a rich man's tomb. All this happened as the Lord God gave Isaiah the picture to write, and even that early the Scripture tells the people he will be despised and rejected, but Jesus did not stay in that rich man's tomb, He came out of that tomb the third day and now has returned to Heaven to make intercession for us. In other words, He is our go-between and goes to God for us. Have you talked to Him today? He is waiting to hear from each of us.

Read: John 14:3 and John 14:27

Do you feel alone and as if all your loved ones have forsaken you today? We live in a day of people staying so busy they do not take time to say "I love you", and this should not be. As we go about our daily routine do we realize there are people who live alone, people who need just a smile or a hug to let them know you care. When Jesus walked on this earth He showed love to all people. There were lepers, crippled ones, those sick for many years, and He healed them all treating them the same, showing He cared. If you feel alone, I would say having a "pity party" today, look around you.

There are many less fortunate and if you know Jesus Christ, you are most wealthy, and you have a friend that sticketh closer than a brother, because He walks with you and He is with you all the time. He loves each of us the same and He gives us a choice to accept Him as our personal Savior and Lord. If you do not know Him, you are missing His fellowship and also the assurance of everlasting life in Heaven. If you are feeling "down" today, look to Jesus, asking Him to lift you up and show you someone who needs your encouragement, then, if you belong to Him, get busy about the Father's business

Read: Luke 2:41-43 & 46-49

*T*his is the beginning of the fall season and we see God's handiwork in all the changing of the climate. We see the beauty of gold, brown and some green that is mixed into the beautiful picture shown us by God. The cycles come each year showing us God never changes. He is the same yesterday, today and forever. He shows us His love by the beauty around us. When we see the colors change as though the finger of God has painted the beautiful landscape, do we think of Heaven and how beautiful it will be. This is the place prepared for us when we die, if we belong to Jesus, if we have asked Him to forgive us and taken Him as our Lord and Savior.

Heaven will have a street of pure gold, and a river as clear as crystal and all the beauty is too fantastic to imagine. So, when we look out our window or drive down a road lined with the beauty of the changing leaves, let us remember God is giving us this beauty to enjoy and he loves each of us. See Him in the picture of autumn and enjoy His Love. If you are feeling down, look up because God is in control.

Read: Daniel 2:20 & 21

When other people look at you and me what do they see? Do they see an unhappy person that is ready to disagree with everyone around him or her? Do they see a kindness and the love of Jesus shinning in your face. When the children of Israel wandered in the wilderness God revealed himself to the people in a cloud, but when Moses met Him face to face the Glory of God shown on face so brightly he had to wear a veil. When we speak face to face with God, really pray before Him, our entire countenance should show we know Him, depend on Him and have been with Him.

One of the old songs we sung years ago was, "Let Others See Jesus in You" and its message was "keep telling the story." When we are at work today, will people know we are Christians? Will they know we trust Him by our actions and our attitudes? As Paul traveled, preaching Jesus, he always gave thought to the way he would be perceived, and his biggest concern was whether others would see Jesus in him. We, as Christians, are to be the light of the world. Did you know you might be the only Bible someone will read today? We are not to "give up" because Jesus will walk with us through every situation.

Read: 2nd Corinthians 4:1-3

"Jesus paid it all, all to Him I owe." We have sung these words many times, but are we, after conversion, supposed to sit down and say, "Jesus paid it all, there is nothing for me to do? We know Jesus brought salvation to this world. His resurrection assured each of us of eternal life in Heaven if we will accept Him. He gave us a gift no other person on earth could give us, because He is the perfect Son of God and was willing to die, shedding His blood for us. So, when we are born again, some might say adopted into the family of God, do we sit and say "I am going to Heaven and there is nothing more for me to do, I have no worries?" This is not the way Lottie Moon, missionary to China in the nineteenth century talked of our responsibility. The prime object of of course is forgiveness of sin, but then we are to follow in the footsteps of Jesus. We are to reach out to others with His message. You might say, "I am not a preacher or Missionary, so I cannot do this?" How do you talk to your co-workers each day? How do you treat your family?

How do people see you when you are not in a church pew? Do you show Jesus in the way you talk and in your everyday walk? Do you testify of Him with a Christian influence? Many people in the world are lost and in need of Jesus. They need to see His light in you. There are tracts you might mail with your bills each month, and there are those who need a telephone call.

Read: Romans 10:13 & 14

Would you like to be a mentor to a young christian? The age of a person does not make him or her an old christian. There are those who accepted Jesus Christ a number of years ago and remain a "babe" in Christ. The reason for this could be laziness or it could be they had no-one to encourage them to study their Bible, pray and seek the leadership of God in their life. There are many that do not know the Old Testament is completed by the New Testament and the entire Bible is important to study. Barnabas shows us a model mentor. He befriended Saul, who had been the great persecutor of Christians, when he became converted. When we look at the Scriptures, we see Saul having Christians dragged out of their homes, beaten, and imprisoned.

Jesus Christ changed the man when He met him on the road to Damascus and because of those who believed in his conversion, he became a great Missionary. We find Barnabas going with Saul (now Paul) to preach the Word to unbelievers. When Paul would not accept John Mark for a missionary journey, because for some reason he had turned back on a previous journey, we find Barnabas taking him. The young man, John Mark, later wrote one of the Books of the Bible. Have you encouraged someone to be all they can be in their Christian life? There are those who are "babes" in Christ who need attention. Let us be aware and become a mentor for the Glory of God.

Read: Acts 9:26-30

"*T*he Lord is my Shepherd, I shall not want." What does it mean? What is God telling His Children? We live in a time when we have so much and we want more. That is, more of the worldly goods. You might say, "I want the finest car, the best house, the finest clothes." This is not at all the message of the Psalm. God has told us He will supply all our needs, according to His riches in Glory. Wants and needs are different. Children want the same expensive shoes their classmates have because it is human to want. Jesus is talking about walking with us, talking with us, leading us and being there for us to pray to Him at any time day or night. He will care for us as a shepherd cares for his sheep, leading us in the good paths and showing us the peace that passes all understanding. When we have Jesus as our Shepherd we will have no fear.

Look at the saints in the Scriptures who were willing to die for the cause of Christ. They had no fear because they knew Jesus would be awaiting them in Heaven. In Luke Chapter 12, as Jesus was teaching, instead of having his mind on the message a man asked Jesus to tell his brother to divide the inheritance with him. His mind was on his wants and Jesus said, "beware of covetousness, a man's life does not consist of the things He possesses." The Savior would have us place our minds on heavenly things and not on greed and material wants of this world.

Read: Psalm 23

*D*o you have trouble understanding the Trinity? Did you know that your salvation involves all three persons of the Trinity? Also we need to realize that salvation, the free gift of eternal life extends back through time and we find this in verse in John 1:1 "In the beginning was the Word (Jesus) and the Word was with God and the Word was God." God the Father selected us for His grace (unearned favor)God the Son offered Himself as a sacrifice for our sin. He paid our penalty or we might say as we were in bondage (slavery) to Satan, Jesus bought us with His Blood., and we are forgiven, free, washed clean in His Blood. We have been "sealed" in Christ by God the Holy Spirit.

When we look at the beautiful handiwork of God, we see everything done in an orderly way. Before Jesus ascended He told His disciples God would send a comforter in His name,which is the Holy Ghost to teach you and He will abide with you forever. In other words Jesus knew He was going back to the Father and He also knew how human it is for us to miss a person we love when they are gone. But He wanted His disciples and us to know he would wait in Heaven, after preparing a beautiful place for each person who belongs to Him.

Read: John 14:27

God gives second chances. Every individual has the need to be given a second chance many times in life. We have the case study of John Mark. He found himself spurned by Paul because he had gone home to Jerusalem instead of continuing to Asia Minor. In this case, was John Mark to give up and say, "I messed up and now God cannot use me." This certainly was not the case because someone came to him, and this tells us that God will send someone to help us through these times.

We know there are no perfect people and we all come short of the Glory of God and except for the shed Blood of Jesus Christ we would all be lost and there would be no second chances to make things right. When he did not fold because of his blunder, John Mark became a special gift to the early church. Later we see him traveling with Paul on Missionary journeys and even writing one of the Books of the New Testament. We see Paul, who later valued John Mark, asking for him to be brought to him, saying he was valuable in his ministry. Second Chances.... We all need them and God has made a way for us to be forgiven and will give us a new life of service to Him.

Read: Acts 13:13 and Acts 15:37-39

*W*hen we look at the news on TV or listen via radio, is it not easy to say, "God, you see the trouble we are in, where are you?" God is in the same place He has always been, but what about America? Christians are being threatened on every side. We are being told what to believe, and God's Word is left out. We have people trying to take God out of everything we have. With Christmas coming up you will hear people in stores saying "Happy Holiday" instead of Merry Christmas. Jesus' Birthday is forgotten and the idea of gifts is first in most minds. This is just one of the ways we, in America have left God out of our lives. The terrorists are vowing to take over all Christians and wipe them out, even in Rome.

God help us to come to our senses in America and call upon God. We have millions in America who say they are Christians. Let us each look at the Scripture, arise from our slumber and worship the one true God. He should be to each person who belongs to him, Jehovah Jirah, or our provider. Do we care enough to go and worship the Lord? Do we really humble ourselves and pray, realizing God is on His throne? Read: 2nd Chronicles 7:14 and remember that God is the same yesterday and today and forever. When He makes a promise, it is sure.

Read: 2nd Chronicles 7:14

*D*o you wonder why God allows you to go through the troubles and trials you have, when you belong to Him? Our Sunday School lessons have been in the Book of Genesis and we see Joseph, a spoiled son by his father. Even though the father has eleven other sons Joseph is the one favored, even given a special coat of many colors. If a person has always had everything he wanted, he or she will expect the same treatment through life, and a spoiled person is not fit for the Master's use. He or she will be a selfish individual. God allowed Joseph to go through the fire of troubles, trials, and even temptation so he could be made a useful vessel for Him You see, God had a plan for Joseph's life just as He has a plan for the life of each individual who belongs to Him.

We do not know how much hate and resentment Joseph had to get rid of during the bad times caused by his brothers. We do see God at work molding him into a fine man, a leader who will save his people, and they are Jacob (Israel) and his sons. Do you see, in this story, how God made him a man of forgiveness. God will allow each of us to be refined into pure silver, discarding the dross, to make us vessels He can use. The Blood of Jesus will cleanse us and we will be taught to walk with Him.

Read: Malachi 3:2 & 3

*T*he ultimate purpose of God is the salvation of every person. God said, I have no pleasure in him that dieth". God's character is immeasurable love, profound patience, infinite mercy and eternal righteousness. We are given the "road map" to God many times in the Scriptures. Jesus said, "no man (person) cometh to the Father (God) but by Me." Jesus came to this earth to make a way for a person, when he or she dies to dwell in heaven with Him. My belief is this: When God breathed into man's nostrils, he became a living soul. When he or she dies that soul passes into a spiritual existence, leaving the body behind.

While we are living we choose our destination. God never created robots, but thinking, feeling, responsible human beings. We have a choice to make while we are living on earth and when we draw our final breath we cannot change our destination. There are those who say, " I cannot feel sense of sorrow for the sin, and I have no desire to believe in God." God sends no person to hell.He chooses to go there. I read the story of a person who encountered an old man. His clothes were filthy from lying in the gutter, his jaw was relaxed and mingled with profanity were drunken mumblings. This was the sight of a man who damned himself. Would God forgive Him? Yes, if he would call out to Him, asking Him to forgive and save him, this man could be cleaned up and become a worthwhile life for God on earth and know he has a home in Heaven. It is said of Judas, "he went to his own place", and that was a place he had made for himself.

Read: Matthew 11:28-30

*A*re we consistent with our worship? It doesn't matter what time we stop to worship God each day, He will be waiting to hear from us. What really matters is the fact that we show up regularly. No matter the circumstances surrounding us we are not to give up. During our life our schedules might change many times, but we should never let the time with God slip away from us. consistency doesn't mean perfection, but it does mean you refuse to give up. So, if you have to change your time to talk with God, that is alright, He is waiting in any place and at any time.

When we spend time with the Lord we will come away invigorated, knowing we are loved and feel the joy of His presence. This is SO important, we all need to meet and talk with God on a regular basis. With the troubles brewing in our country, we need strength and wisdom for the days we might face in the future, and He is our source. "From whence comes my help, my help comes from the Lord."

Read: Luke 10:38-42

We need to think on God's Love today. Christianity has been characterized as the religion of love and that is true. Jesus loved us so much He was willing to come to this earth, and die a horrible death that we could be saved. But, let us think of our love. If, in the name of love we uncritically accept every idea or value of others when we know these are against the Word of God, we open ourselves up to error. God never told us to put our brains in neutral when it comes to the matter of faith. We hear people use the word love in different ways, today. "I love my pet", "I love my spouse", "I love a certain food" or my children, my car and many other things. The true meaning of love is when we look in the Bible and see God's love which is: lasting, sacrificial, healing and reconciling, mutual between the Father, Son and the Holy Spirit and effective. It is not just emotions or words, but deeds that benefit people. It is also fearless, discerning, accepting and not condemning. It is generous.

When we search our hearts and the Scriptures, in what ways do we each see our love needs to develop? God, help us to remember that you are the judge and this is not our job. You know each heart and each person who belongs to you, and my job is not to say "this one is belongs to God" or "this one does not"

Read: Luke: 18:10-14

We have many promises from God and they will all come true. But, Satan also promises many things to people who will serve him. He promised Jesus authority over all the kingdoms of the world. We know Satan as the "father of lies." He will tell a partial truth to suck people into a sinful lifestyle. He spoke the truth when he told Jesus, "this has been delivered to me and I can give it to whomever I wish," but notice he did not admit the world powers had been given to him by God Himself., who possessed authority over the entire universe. Jesus did not answer by laying claim to His rightful authority, but answered Satan in a way that would be a lesson to each of us. "Thou shall worship the Lord thy God and Him only shall thou serve." When we look at Jesus' answer we are compelled to ask, "are we to look at the benefits or the costs?"

The benefits of following Satan in this world might be great, making people rich in worldly goods, but to reap these benefits is a person "selling out" our Lord by compromising His commands, His values,or His honor. The cost is much to high when a person listens to Satan. Remember the song, "What Would You Give in Exchange for Your Soul?" The only way is to do as Jesus did and say, "Get thee behind me Satan!", and faithfully follow Jesus' teachings.

Read: Luke 4:5-8

$\mathcal{R}$emember singing "Little is much when God is in it?" We find that God delights in using people who are disadvantaged. Before he was stoned Stephen mentioned three of these people in the Book of Acts. God used Abraham and Sarah, a childless immigrant couple to found the Israelite nation. They were used as a witness to all the nations. God took Joseph from a favored child, sold by his brothers into slave trade and shaped him into a national leader who was able to rescue his family from famine and death. God made Moses into a liberator and a nation builder from a minority child who was marked for slaughter by the Pharaoh.

When we look at God's plan, it is beautiful to behold. All these people would probably have been ignored by us, but God sees what we can become for Him and He has a plan. Saul was busy persecuting the ones called Christian, because they followed Christ. God shows us by his life, there is no person so mean, or so unbelieving that He cannot change them. After conversion we see him as becoming a great missionary. Although Stephen was stoned to death because of his message, we find his testimony and his message lives on as a witness to others. We are never to give up and think we can do nothing for Christ. He has much for each of us to do in this life. Ask Him what He would have you do? When you are shown, do the job with all your strength! Serve Him! When people make fun of you and talk about you, think of Stephen.

Read: Acts: 7:51-56

*A*re we aware of the temptations of Satan? It is no sin to be tempted, but the sin is when we continue to think on a wrong until we find ourselves doing the things we know we should not do, because God's Word teaches us they are wrong. Temptation is tough. It is a test. It is the enticement to do wrong, and God has allowed us to be tempted, because He wants people who choose to serve Him. God could have created us differently, but there would be no joy for Him if we had to trust Him, with no choice. He wants us to love and obey Him.

Temptation may involve great pleasure or illegitimate gains. Temptation is usually attractive to the human being. So, how do we resist the temptations which befall us each day? Have you prayed today, asking God for that strength? When we neglect the study of God's Word and Prayer we are leaving ourselves open to the wiles of Satan. We will gradually get further and further from Him and become weaker Christians, which will leave us open to Satan's snares. Jesus warned His followers to pray so they would not fall into temptation.

Read: Luke 22:39-46

*D*id you know you can be in the bondage of bitterness? There are those who have hurt each of us in the past, but we can rise above the gossips, and those who would use us to salve their egos. So, what is important to you and me? Should we let God cleanse us from all this and look forward to serving Him with a clean and forgiving heart? Everyone could look around and think they have been used or they are being used by others. This is what I call a "pity party" and is not fit for a Christian. We have only one person to look to and that is Jesus Christ. His promise is that He will be with us til the end of the world or He will be with us in this world and when we die He will be awaiting us in Heaven. He will loose the chains of bondage or slavery from you and me.

Do you feel that friends have forsaken you? If you do, forgive and pray for them, then go about your business of serving God each day with a thankful heart. Do you find it hard to forgive someone? If so, we must think about our sins before we cast stones at someone else.

Read: Ephesians 4:31 & 32

We date the doctrine of the Holy Spirit from the day of Pentecost. That was the day when all the disciples and those who had followed Jesus were gathered together. Jesus did not keep the fact that He was going to die from His disciples. He had walked with them, talked with them, guided them and they loved Him. He knew they needed help in this life and He promised not to leave them helpless. The Holy Spirit was to come and be His other Self. He would abide with the Christ followers, guiding them and would be present all the time. Jesus had been on this earth thirty-three years and the night before His crucifixion He has only a few more things to do. He was to die on the cross, be buried and rise again.

On this night His disciples were heavy with sorrow. After being with Jesus for three years, was this the end? Jesus knew the need of promising those that followed Him a Helper. Before He ascended, Jesus told His disciples to remain in Jerusalem and wait for the promise He had given them to come true. The disciples obeyed Jesus and continued in prayer in Jerusalem.

Read: John 14: 16-18

*A*t the heart of the Christian Religion is the cross. We, as believers, should not think of the cross as just a wooden structure on Golgotha's Hill nineteen hundred years ago, but we should think of the reason for the cross. At the very heart of the cross is the spirit of sacrifice. Jesus died on that cross to forgive our Sin, but when we accept His gift of eternal life, we are not to say, "it is done, now I will take my rest." There is a misguided belief that the Christian life is easy. This is not true,because Jesus never promised us an easy road, but He did make the promise that He would be with us always.

There have been many people who have been tested and tried, and yes, lost their lives because they lived and served Jesus Christ. We find story after story of young missionaries like David Livingstone who served in darkest Africa, John Howard giving himself to those in prisons. and many others who gave their lives for Christ. For the world to be saved there are many who have suffered, looking to Jesus and the wonderful, blessed gift He gave on the cross. When a person is saved, he or she should be taught there is work to be done for God. We are called on to deny ourselves, and put Christ first. To refuse what Jesus offered on the cross is to perish, but to accept it is to live. This is the breadth and length of God's Love.

Read: John 3:16

*L*ife is like a journey for each of us. We do not have a "do-over." We should think of this each day and take great care in all we say, all we do and our actions toward others. God has given us the blessing of life and His perfect will is that we will follow His plan for our life during this journey. We will have dark, gloomy times, and there will be rocky roads, and valleys, but when there is a valley there will be a mountain. There, we will have blessings and wonderful experiences in our Christian lives. Jesus never promised us we would have all good times in this life, but He did tell us He would be with us til the end of the world.

We are promised in Isaiah 40:31 that those who wait upon the Lord will have their strength renewed, they will mount up with wings as eagles, and they shall run and not be weary and they shall walk and not faint. When we, who belong to Jesus, find ourselves in a valley because of many different things, let us think of the journey God has given us. We need to pray, seeking the face of God, knowing He is there and hears our prayers. Let us ask God to help us draw strength from our troubles and trails to help others. Help us to become stronger Christians.

Read: 2nd Corinthians 1: 3 & 4

We read of animal sacrifice in the Old Testament and know this is the foreshadow of the sacrifice of Jesus Christ for sin. The blood of animals covered the people's sins for a time and they had to wait until time to go for sacrifice to be forgiven again. When we look at this and realize the burden of sin the people had to carry for months, we will thank Jesus for all He did for us. As we know Jesus, not merely a man, but the Son of God was willing to come to this earth, live among people and go to a cross, suffering more than we can imagine so that each of us will have the freedom to call upon God for forgiveness.

Each person is in the bondage of sin, which means bound by satan until he or she realizes their need for the freedom found in Jesus Christ. Only Jesus, because of the shedding of His precious blood, can forgive us forever. He will clean us up and make us a new creation or we will say He will forgive our sins, washing us clean by His Blood, when we call out to Him, asking Him to forgive us. We will have a different outlook on life if we follow Him. We will realize His love for us and His preparation of a heavenly home for us when we die.

Read: 1st Peter 1: 18-21

November

Joseph was sold into slavery by his brothers. This was a totally unexpected turn, especially in light of the dreams he had recently. In those dreams he was told his family would bow down to him, not sell him. How could becoming the property of wandering traders and sold into slavery fit the plan the dreams told. Had he been imagining all this? Joseph was not imagining, but the things his brothers did to him fit the plans of God for good. Those involved in his mistreatment were not aware of God's hand, He ordered their steps. God knew about all of this ahead of time, and we know when life throws the unexpected at us, it is never unexpected by God. He always has a plan for each of us.

As we look at God's hand and how it applied to Joseph's life, we know He is in the decision making process for each of us. There are times we stress over finding God's will for our lives and it is important to seek His direction for our life. When we go forward in faith, there is no sense in turning back, wondering if we somehow missed His plan. We are to seek God's will and pursue it, aiming at faithfulness, and God will always put our steps (lives) in the order He has planned for us. We might say, "how precious are Thy thoughts unto me, O God! how great is the sum of them" Psalm 139:17. Let go and let God have His wonderful way in our life, today.

Read: Psalm 86:10-13

A Christian is able to read God's Word and see how they should live. We do not have the excuse of "I did not know", but the truth is this: we have a spiritual obligation to live for Jesus, thanking Him, loving Him day by day. We all love comfort and there are many times when serving God is not comfortable. Maybe we will be called upon to help someone at night when we would be much more comfortable in our bed, snuggled under the covers. How comfortable do we think Jesus was when He was in the Garden of Gethsemane? While the disciples, putting their comfort first, slept Jesus prayed.

How many times in our lives have we selfishly shunned the hardships for our own comforts? When God provides comfort for us, we should thank Him for all His goodness, but there will be times when He will call us to get out of our comfort zone to serve Him. In other words we are called when the need arises to put God's work first. We can forego some of the good in order to have the very best and that means having Jesus who will give us blessings beyond measure and life to the fullest. After the crucifixion Peter went fishing, doing the thing he liked, but Jesus later asked Him, "do you love Me."

Read: John 21:15-17

*J*esus taught many times in parables and they were beautiful lessons. The parable of the lost coin is one that we might skip over if we are not careful. More than likely this lost coin was the woman's wedding coin. She is searching diligently for the coin that is lost. We see her sweeping the house and looking into every nook and corner and finally she sees something glitter and there is the coin. Most of the time the emphasis is put upon the woman searching, but when we think of the coin we see it has not lost its value. It is not a bad coin, but one that has been misplaced. Since it was misplaced it could not fulfil its function, for which it was made. This coin was in useless isolation and concealment. Jesus was teaching that man was created to function within the will of God, but like the coin and the prodigal son, when a person is under self will and desires he or she is tragically misplaced.

A story is told of a woman attending a revival meeting, going forward, saying she wanted to become a Christian, but she could not because she hated a person who had mistreated her. She was told to forgive and she would be forgiven but her reply was, "Never!" A Christian can be misplaced and find his or her way back to Jesus Christ, by calling on Him, asking forgiveness, giving up the selfwill and beginning a life that will be useful to Him Notice Jesus saying "there will be joy in the presence of angels when one sinner repenteth."

Read: Luke 15:8-10

Calvary, the death of death. What a strange sentence, but the truth of what Jesus did for each person who will accept His gift of eternal life. We think of the cross and we mutter, "He was wounded for my transgressions, He was bruised for my iniquities and by His stripes I am healed." Then we think of His statement, "And I, if I be lifted up from the earth will draw all men unto me". People did not know what this prediction of Jesus meant until He was lifted up from the earth on a cross to be crucified. He was the only one who was perfect and could redeem us and He went willingly,offering Himself for each person who will choose to accept Him. Jesus saw that the world was wrong and He knew the human race was in bondage or we might say enslaved by Satan, and He cared enough to go to the cross for you and for me. We think of the song stating "the love of Christ, how rich and pure, how marvelous and strong" and then the next statement, "it shall forever more endure."

The story is told of a dying boy, years ago, when medical knowledge was not perfected as much as it is today. The boy was pale and his people knew he had only hours to live, but one aunt said, "I believe if he had a blood transfusion, he would live. The next day, after the blood was given, the boy became much better and lived to serve God. Life is in the blood and Jesus willingly gave His blood for us. Let us be thankful and bless His Name.

Read: Luke 23:33

*W*e sing a song "How Great is Our God". We should ask ourselves this question today. Do we stop to realize God controls everything. Even though Satan is given power in this world, God can stop him at any time. Why do we pray? We pray because we know our heavenly Father will hear our petitions. You might ask, "why, then did He not let this person get well and answer our plea for that person to continue living. We might even say, "why, God, did you let this or that happen to my loved one?"

We do not know the mind of God. Many times He takes a loved one home to be with Him because it is time for that person to be free of suffering. We, human beings, do not see this because we think selfishly. We want our loved ones to remain with us. We want to hug them, see them, and just know they are with us. We are not thinking about the beautiful home that has been prepared and the fact there will be no more pain. Do you remember the song, "Let go and Let God have His wonderful way." We, as Christians, need to earnestly pray for God's Will to be done , being willing to accept His will, and everything will be alright.

Read: John 11:25 & 26

We, as Christians, are often accused of cramming our belief down another's throat. We might talk all day and we cannot convert another person. When we get the idea that our responsibility is conversion we are totally wrong. The Holy Spirit is the only One who converts people. Even though we are responsible for letting our light shine before others that they will see our walk with the Lord, we have nothing more to do with their salvation. When a loved one did not respond to your testimony, did you feel that you had failed?

We do not measure our success by those who listen to us. If failure was the case, let us look at the life of Jesus. He preached and taught many people and some listened and responded, but others did not. We might look at the parable of the different kinds of soils, and think of ourselves as farmers. We are to sow good seed and nurture whatever faith sprouts. Many people accept Jesus, and want to live for Him, but no person takes the time to help them grow by teaching, encouraging and loving them. We need to make our experience with God available to others and that includes our failures as well as our mountain-top experiences. Find someone who needs you today and mentor them. There are many new Christians out there who need you. Once an evangelist was asked if a person was his convert, and the reply was this, "must be, if he was God's, he wouldn't act like this."

Read: John 6:64-67

*H*ow many things in this life can you say you are absolutely sure of? We know things might change in a day or in an hour, but there is One we can be sure of and that is Jesus. The words to a song is this: "Blessed assurance, Jesus is mine! Oh what a foretaste of glory divine. Heir of salvation, purchase of God, born of His Spirit, washed in His Blood." What a beautiful message!

We look at God's creation and we know He will send the morning, rain or shine and we know He will cause the seasons to change, but beyond that few things are certain in this life. Many disappointments come and promises are broken, but we can be sure of one thing. If we have accepted the gift of salvation Jesus provided for us on the cross, asked Him to forgive us our sin and turned our life over to Him, no man can take this gift from us. We are able to say "Jesus is mine" He is my strength from day to day, He hears me when I pray and He has sent the Holy Spirit to teach and guide me through the rest of my life.

Read: John 14:1-4

$\mathcal{T}$here is no need for a Christian to speak of their work for God, because the most important thing is to "walk the walk" instead of "talk the talk." Nothng is done in the darkness that God doesn't see. Jesus told the Pharisees they wanted to be seen of men, they wanted the uppermost or the most prominent seats in gatherings. They thought they were more religious than anyone else, and maybe they were religious, but was their religion of God? No, their teaching was "act to be seen of others" or we would say hypocritical. (putting on an act) Jesus warned the people to beware of the leaven of the Pharisees and the leaven He was speaking of was hypocrisy. In the same Chapter in Luke 12, Jesus told the people that God even knew the numbers of hairs on their heads.

We realize we are all unworthy of His love, but the blood of Jesus Christ will wash us clean and make us vessels or cups that are not just cleaned up on the outside, but also from within. We have nothing to brag about, but we can exalt Jesus Christ and what He has done for us. We, each, need to commune with Him, walking with Him daily.

Read: Matt. 6:5-7

We think of self improvement. We use different equipment to get our bodies in better shape. That is good, but what about our spiritual growth? We measure ourselves by our actions and as long as we are doing more we think of ourselves as improving spiritually. But God looks at us in a different light. He looks at the motives. Remember the Pharisees and the religious leaders of Jesus' day. Their deeds were right but their motives were wrong. The outward behavior, is very important but it can be ruined by misplaced intent.

God wants internal integrity, not a "look at me and all my goodness attitude." God calls for a close examination of our intentions. Are we acting out of self interest or do we truly have a passion for God and His Kingdom? If we ask Him, the Holy Spirit will shine a heavy dose of reality into the hidden purposes of our hearts. Dr A.W. Tozer said, "It is not what a man does that determines whether his work is sacred or secular, it is why he does it."

Read: Proverbs 16:2 & 3 and Psalm 139:23 & 24

Our Pastor brought us a good message on duty this week. What is your duty as a Christian or my duty? Are we to live our lives selfishly, not caring or even thinking of anyone else? I heard one person make this amusing statement, "You are not saved to sit down and sit, but to get up and git." There is much truth in this even if is not worded properly. There is much to be done on this earth and Jesus left His followers to witness to others by word and deed.

How much do you study God's Word? In His Word we find the Word of Life and also the answer to questions we might have about serving Him. There was one who asked God for wisdom instead of riches of the world and he became the wisest man we know. When he wrote the Book of Ecclesiastes in the last chapter he said this, "the conclusion of the whole matter is to fear God and keep His commandments, for this is the whole duty of man." Our Pastor brought this out in a way that all could understand. His statement was this: "Just do what God says." If we do not study His Word we will not know what God says or what He wants us to do.

Read: Matthew 28:19 & 20

*T*here is no way a person can get away from the eyes of God. He sees our actions, knows our thoughts and intentions. We have many examples in God's Word to prove this and they are to make us think on the "all seeing" eye of God. In the Book of Numbers we find a Prophet of God wanting material gain but he would not curse Israel because He knew God forbade it. Jonah recognized the voice of God but did not want to obey. He tried to run, but God knew where he was all the time. As we get into the New Testament we see Paul wanting to preach in Asia Minor, but God, speaking through the Holy Spirit would not let him go to the place he wanted to go, but directed him to Europe. Each of these people had plans, but these plans did not meet with the agenda God had for them. So it is with us.

We determine which direction we want to go and God might intervene. God's Will is not to be usurped. The question is this: will we be flexible and seek to fulfill His Will or will we stubbornly seek to defy it. We cannot see the future, but the all-seeing eye of God sees and knows about all our tomorrows. We, as Christians, should open our hearts and say, "Lord, wherever you lead, I will go" and as the song says, "Let go and let God have His wonderful way."

Read: Proverbs 16:9 & John 10:27

*H*ave you ever thought about sharing something with the sun? We rise each morning, like sun to display the glory of God's sustaining and creative power. We rise each morning and if we are Christians, we are to display the glory of Christ, who lives within us, through the day. Think about this: The sun warms the earth, and we should radiate the warmth of God's Love. That is the reason we are created. God wanted a creation He could have fellowship with, who would show His love to the entire world.

We need to realize the fact that everything we do and everything we say either gives God the glory due His Name or shows a rebellious creation, a person who is bringing reproach on the name of Jesus Christ. Let us be aware that we are to be careful with our influence, because someone is watching our lives. Be careful to honor God in all you do. He died for you and me.

Read: 2nd Corinthians 4:6

How many times do you pray and feel that God is not listening because you have seen or heard no answer to your prayer? In this life we have many periods of waiting. A couple might have prayed for a child for a long time and finally they realize they will have one, but they have to wait for nine months before the arrival of the child. A child wants to become an adult and go out on his or her own or maybe go to college, but they have to wait and study for years to reach that goal.

Before Jesus went away He told His disciples to wait in Jerusalem for the promised Holy Spirit, which they did. Thinking on these things,we need to ask God to give us the patience to wait for His perfect will to be done in our lives. Our final goal will be at the end of this earthly life and a beautiful, eternal home in Heaven. Blessings are awaiting each of us,who belong to Him, but we must learn to keep praying to God to work all things out and patiently wait on Him Remember, when you pray, God does answer your prayer, but the answer is not always the one we think we want. He might say yes, no, or wait awhile.

Read: Isaiah 40:31

We read of the parable of the rich man and he is called the rich fool. When you read it, notice how many times he uses the word I. He is only depending on himself. I made this crop and I will use it as I want to or save it as I think. When God blessed him so much, he had no room to store his grain, he never once thanked him or did he think of anyone who might have a need. God calls him a fool, because he was only thinking of his living for years to come.

We do not know how many years we are granted, so isn't is wiser to serve God, thanking Him for His blessings as we go from day to day. Our society has put Thanksgiving on the back burner, so to speak, because the materialistic greed has become so great that people begin advertising for Christmas in October. We allow Thanksgiving to be overshadowed with shopping. Sure, Christmas is to be celebrated, but we need to stop and thank God for all His blessings through the year, and when the time comes, we need to thank Him for the birth of His Son. During this time we need to remember whose birthday it is, and teach our children about Jesus.

Read: Luke 12:16-20

*T*here is a human hunger in people to please God. Many times the thought of sacrifice makes a person think they have pleased him. When we look into His Word we see God ask the question, "To what purpose is the multitude of sacrifices to me?" The people were coming to their gatherings with animals to sacrifice and they were offering oblations that were useless. Why were they useless? God is telling the people He is weary of them coming with vain worship.

It is an abomination to live for Satan all week and go to church on Sunday, putting on a act as though you have worshiped for days. Satan loves that lifestyle in people, because he is full of lies and deceit and he knows if he can get a person who says they are Christian to live in this lifestyle they will influence many others to do the same. This will hinder the work of God and cause those who are searching to lose confidence in the Church. When I say the Church, I am talking about the group of people who call themselves God's people.

Read: Isaiah 1:16-20

I think forgiveness is the hardest task for the Christian. Jesus has told us to be forgiven, we have to forgive others. When I think of Him and the horrible way He was treated, beaten with a cat of nine tails which was leather thongs with stones and glass and sharp objects in them, I realize we would not have recognized Him. Other men would have been killed with this treatment, but our Lord was to die on the cross.

Do not look at a picture of an artist' version and think Jesus looked like this when he went to the cross. He was spit upon and even had his beard plucked out, and the shame was terrible. Yet, Jesus prayed, "Father, forgive them, they know not what they do." Jesus showed us how to forgive others no matter what they do to us. A Christian's heart should be soft, compassionate and forgiving, always ready to show Christ in us.

Read: Matthew 5:43-48

*T*here are many who say you do not have to have education to serve God. This is true because there are people in all walks of life who need to hear God's Word. How will I be able to tell them if I have not studied, if I have not learned from the Scriptures?

We look at Moses and know he spent the first 40 years of his life in the Pharoah's court. He was taught all the knowledge of the Egyptians. This probably included religion, Science, literature, geometry and many other subjects. The next forty years God had other things for him to learn. He spent these years in the desert studying animals and herding sheep. There, God was able to speak to Him, giving him the vast job of freeing his people. Saul and the pharisees fell into the trap of much learning and they hid behind this so as not to deal with the will of God.

What should we do in today's society? We should learn all we can so that we will be able to answer questions, asked us, about God's Word.

Read: 2nd Timothy 3:14-17

*I*f we belong to Jesus, we are adopted into the family of God. When a child is adopted he or she is chosen and they belong to the parent or parents forever. This is the way it is with a child of God, and sometimes that child gets out of line and God sees and knows and yes, corrects him or her. There is an old song and in this song I remember the words, "There's an all-seeing eye watching you." The way we live each day is known to God.

When children are growing up they might hide things from their parents but not so with God. There is no hiding from Him. Do we realize the fact that God, even when we are in a dangerous situation, is with us in the storms, as we had yesterday, when we cannot see to drive for the rain, and He is always with us in the storms of life. If someone has hurt you or wronged you, instead of trying to take revenge, run to God with the hurt. He is available to listen to you night or day. Jesus does not want His brothers and sisters to live in fear.

He wants peace for us and we can have it by depending on Him.. There is the story of the storm when the disciples were in the ship with Jesus and He was asleep. They ran to Him.

Read: Mark 4:37-41

We are facing the same situation in America, today, the people faced long ago. Christians are in a minority and people are saying "it is politically incorrect to say Jesus saves." Every time we see persecution, we see it coming from the religious people. When I say religious people, I might be talking about any religion.

There are many religions in the world, today, but Jesus plainly told us, "I am the way the truth and the Life, no man comes to the Father but by Me" He also said, "Fear not, little flock for it is the Father's good pleasure to give you the kingdom." For the Christian, Jesus is the Shepherd and we follow Him, but there are many that do not accept Jesus as God's Son.

When Stephen was stoned, his opponents came from a group of people who called themselves freedmen. This was a religious center in Jerusalem and the people were known as Hellenists. They claimed to be religious and said that Stephen was speaking blasphemous words, stirring up the people into a riot. He was teaching Jesus and they did not believe in Him.

Read: Acts 6:9-15

$\mathcal{D}$id you know false teachers can sway people who are saved? We find in Acts chapter 15, the accounting of Paul and Barnabas returning to Antioch and reporting the good news that God had opened the door of faith to the Gentiles. Now, men who claimed to speak for the church came saying in order for them to be saved they had to become Jews. The claims were this: The Gentiles had to accept the culture trends of Hebrew religion and reject their ethnic backgrounds. In other words, these people were wanting to add works to faith and this is no good. These false doctrines have continued to trouble the church (those who truly believe in Jesus Christ as Lord and Savior) until this day.

There is nothing to be added to believing and accepting Jesus Christ as Lord and Savior. When a person comes to Him, sincerely sorrow for their sins and ask Him, He will forgive and they are immediately added to the family of God. A person cannot work to earn salvation or pay their way. So, you might ask, why do we work and why do we tithe? These things are done in obedience to Jesus who loved us so much He went to the cross to buy our pardon. They are done because we do belong to Him. Yes, we are to live our lives for Jesus and a true Christian wants to do this.

Read: Hebrews 10:10-14

*T*oday we will think of commitment. This is something we want even acknowledge because the cost might be too great. Today convenience usually wins out. I will do this or that if it is convenient and if I have the extra time. People were the same in Jesus' day. As He began to unfold a new way of life, He was challenged on the marriage vows. After Jesus talked about boundless forgiveness, the discussion of divorce came up. Jesus did not ignore the problems and failures of human relationships.

The short comings of human beings are the very things that make commitment and forgiveness a critical part of the Christian's life. Next we find the man who wanted to secure eternal life. He did not mind keeping the rules he had been taught all his life, but when it came time for him to commit his money, he went away sorrowful. We should remember the Scripture, "I am the Lord your God, Thy shall have no God before Me." Christians should take care and not put anything before your commitment to God. It could be your children, your house, pleasure, money and many other things. Commit everything to Him. He is to be first.

Read: Ephesians 6:10-13

We look into the Scriptures and find Jesus dealing with people where they were and on their terms. He met Nicodemus at night and the woman of Samaria at midday. Jesus will meet with you at any time of the day and at any place and He wants to meet with, and commune with you. We need to follow His example of being no respecter of persons. He shunned none, but showed only love to all peoples. All the time Jesus walked on this earth, He was a model for us. He showed us, by His life, how we should live, work and communicate the Gospel Message. You might ask, "How will I be able to follow the footsteps of Jesus?"

We each have different abilities. These abilities are the tools, so to speak, that Jesus has given each person to use in this life. Some are able to preach, sing, teach, show compassion to the down-trodden, nurse the sick and there are many more things I could mention. We are never to say, "I have nothing to give". We see two very different people. We see the samaritan woman, who had lived a scandalous lifestyle, despised by her community because of the way she had lived. When she met Jesus she was a changed individual. We see Nicodemus apparently never openly identified with Jesus until after His crucifixion when he helped prepare the body for burial. You will notice Jesus confronted him about being born again and then He let him go away. Jesus told people by His words and His lifestyle and that is what we are to do. There are many ways people responded.some after they were fed, some after they were healed, and some after they saw the resurrected Christ.

Read: John 3: 17 &18

*H*ave you ever heard a person ask, "How do I know God will forgive me?" "I have done some bad things and I just don't think He will forgive?" Yes, He will forgive anything a person has done. How do I know? Because the Bible tells me He will. Not only are we told in the Scriptures God will forgive, but we are also told He will cast our sin far from us, to be remembered no more. When a person makes a decision to come to Jesus Christ and live for Him, his or her sin of rebellion will be forgiven. When I say the sin of rebellion, I am talking about rebelling against the teachings of God. The sin of rebellion is this: "I do not need God, I will live my own life as I please". After a person accepts Jesus, he or she knows they have been washed clean in the Blood Jesus shed and then they want to live for Him.

When we come to Jesus we must have forgiveness in our hearts for those who have wronged us. We cannot let a grudge stand between us and God. When we look at the model prayer, the first thing we see is this: "Our Father, who art in Heaven, Hallowed be Thy Name. Thy kingdom come, Thy will be done in earth as it is in Heaven. Give us this day our daily bread and forgive us our debts as we forgive our debtors." We have to believe God will do as He says and even David said, "Blessed are they whose iniquities are forgiven, and whose sins are covered."

Read: Ephesians 1: 6 & 7

Do you remember the song, "He Hideth My soul." When we think of the words , "and covers me there with His Hand," we can picture God hiding us on a mountain side that is rocky and we see an indention or a cleft in the rock and think of God hiding us in there from the hands of Satan. Then we think of God's great Hand covering us. I think this is a most beautiful picture of the love of God. We think of our parents and how they protected us, warning us of danger and taking care of our needs, but their abilities were limited. Not so with God, He is in control of all the universe. He has warned us we would not be trouble free in this life, but He has also promised to be with us. walk with us, comfort us in our troubled times and guide us through this life.

We must think of God, our Heavenly Father, who wants to give us good things, love us, and He is always present for us to commune with Him. Jesus, our Mediator, or we could say "go between" prays to the Father for us. We see how much He cares when we think of Him leaving His Heavenly Home and coming to this earth to be born of a Virgin, growing up in a poor home, and going to the cross so we can be saved. How thankful I am that Jesus cares for you and me. Read His Prayer for us before He was hung on the Cross. This is the Lord's Prayer. It is a prayer of intercession for us.

Read: John 17: 9-15

The greatest motivating factor in the search for freedom is this: People want to be free to choose. We are free in this great country to choose to worship as we please and this is a great blessing, we need to thank God that we have a choice. Many soldiers have fought and died so we could have this freedom, which many countries do not have. When we are born, because of Adam and Eve, we are born with a sin nature, so this makes us a slave to sin. Jesus Christ came to free us from that bondage. He was willing to die on a cross, shed His blood, so we could have the free gift of salvation. When a person accepts Jesus as Lord and Savior he or she is bought out of the bondage of sin and given eternal life.

There are many who think they have to work to go to Heaven. This is not true. The gift Jesus gave us is free. You might ask, "why, then do Christians sacrifice their time going to worship and doing good for others?" When a person comes to Jesus and realizes the great sacrifice He made for each of us, we serve Him because we have a desire to serve Him. He has freed us from the slavery of sin and He has gone to prepare a beautiful home in Heaven for us when we die. He has given us life eternal. We want to live a life in obedience to Him. This is true freedom.

Read: Romans 6:10-14

*P*aul speaks of our works for God being tried by fire. He uses the term, as a medal being purified in a fire to melt it so the dross or we would say the worthless impurities that are no good can be taken away leaving a pure medal. This is a picture of the Christian, when he or she stands before God to give an account of our works. This evaluation will not be for salvation, but for the worth of our lives on earth. There is a song that says "will there be any stars in my crown" and I do not like to hear it, because the Bible does not say there will be stars in our crowns, but we will have crowns to toss at the feet of Jesus. We will stand at the Judgement Seat of Christ to give an accounting of our lives, if we belong to Jesus. If a person does not belong to Jesus they will stand at the great white throne. In other words, those who stand here are doomed forever. We might ask "will my works be burned up with nothing left of them?" If we serve Jesus with hidden motives as "making a show of our works for others to see" or for personal gain, or popularity, our works are no good in the sight of God.

The Scripture tells us they will be as dirty rags. The right motive is this: We should serve the Lord our God because we love Him and want to please Him. We should live our lives in such a way we will be a testimony or example of Christian service. We might look at it like this: Whatever is left after the fire burns down, are the works we will be rewarded for. Let each of us search ourselves today. Do I serve Jesus with the right motives, knowing He came to earth and suffered a horrible death so that I could have eternal life in Heaven?

Read: 1st Corinthians 3:10-15

$\mathcal{H}$appy Thanksgiving Season to all who read this devotion. We have so much to be thankful for this morning. Count your Many Blessings, Name them one by one. Count your many Blessings and see what God has done." How many times have we sung this? We, can each, stop and look on our lives and see the times God has been with us through sorrow, through sickness, and through many troubles. Have we stopped to realize it was God's Hand leading us through this life? The Bible tells us to "Be still and know that I am God." (Psalm 46:10)

We know, in life we have troubled times but we have the promise of God's Presence. "Yea though I walk through the valley of the shadow of death, Thou art with me." (Psalm 23) We need to stop and think on God this day, thanking Him for His many good gifts and His presence with each of us, who belong to Him.

Read: James 1:17, Matt. 7:11

*H*ave you ever been afraid or do you dwell on the things that might happen that causes you to fear. Every culture seems to be afraid of something or someone. The Hebrews feared the Romans because of their occupation troops. In recent years we look into history and see the west feared the Russians were going to destroy them with nuclear missiles. We cannot ignore physical threats and today we are on the alert even when we go shopping for someone who wants to take advantage of us by robbing us. We are alarmed by the growing drug and gang violence we see on the news each day, and the terrorist we hear about. Satan is alive and well on planet earth, but he is not king.

We need to look at things from the view Jesus gave us. He talks of the fear of the Lord. He is not talking about a fawning, cringing dread that keeps us wallowing in anxiety, but a respect for who God is. He is the one who holds the ultimate power. When we stop and think on Him, it puts our thinking in a proper framework. We see His holiness, righteousness and love. We can't ignore the physical threats and violence, but above all we dare not ignore God who holds our eternal destiny in His Hands. Talk to Him, Call out to Him each day, He is the all powerful One. He has promised He will be with us through it all.

Read: Luke 21:25-28 & Matt. 28: 19 & 20

People think of love today in a way that is confusing and when we think of the ways the word is used, we see a concept in the minds of people that is wrong. The word is used to describe different relationships. Some might say "I love my car," "I love this pizza," "I love my animals," or "I love my companion." What can love possibly mean if it is applied equally to cars, food, dogs or companions? When Jesus recalled the greatest of commandments, both which had to do with love, He was calling for agape love which is a sustained and conscious choice to serve God and also to serve others not expecting repayment. God loved us first, so much, Jesus was willing to die so we could obtain salvation, once for all, without trying to appease God with animal sacrifices, as was done in the past.

God's love allows us to love by choice. We, as Christ followers are to love and forgive, even in the face of rejection. Look around you, there are many sad people at this time of year who need a smile, helping hand, a hug, and encouragement. Have you looked to see, who around you, needs compassion and kindness? Remember, when you read the 13th Chapter of 1st Corinthians to say love where you see the word charity.

Read: 1st Corinthians 13:1-8

We read in the Book of Acts of a man named Simon who thought he could buy the power of God. His quest for power is the very same that drives so many to want power, today. We see it in the political arena, in all our public places, and alas, we also see it in churches. Even among Christians there is a tendency to create power figures. This can be among singers, preachers, writers or any leaders in our churches. But the power of God has nothing to do with earthly acclaim. We don't know what finally happened to Simon who tried to buy the power of God, but we do know he took a sharp rebuke from Peter.

To live for God, one must change our motives and attitudes. The old way of thinking and acting must give away to a new and changed life. Simon may have changed his ways, because we see his plea for mercy and we know if he went to Jesus with this, he was forgiven. We do know previously Simon practiced sorcery and claimed to be a great man. Without Jesus Christ in our lives we are nothing, but when we accept His love and forgiveness we are adopted into the family of God, a joint-heir with Jesus.

Read: Acts 8:18-24

December

You will hear many myths about Christianity, today. We know that the word Christian came into existence when the people followed Christ They were first called Christians at Antioch (Acts 11:26) Jesus taught the greatest moral and spiritual principles ever known and He showed us we should live them. He is the true example we are to follow, not another person. Jesus said, "Love your enemies, lay down your life for others," and He forgave those who crucified Him. He owned no worldly goods except the clothes on His back and was (and still is) the most remarkable teacher of all teachers. One of the myths you will hear today is this: "Oh yes, He was a great moral teacher." What they are saying is that Jesus was only a good man and a great teacher, and nothing more.

When the gospel is left out of the message we have nothing. The gospel is this: Jesus Christ, the Son of God left Heaven and came to earth, born of a virgin , lived among men, was crucified, shedding His precious blood for the sins of people and rose again the third day and went back to Heaven to prepare a place for those who would choose to follow Him. He came to become our Mediator (go-between) to God. He carries our petitions to the Father. Do you know the Love of God? If not, please stop and realize what He has done for each of us.

Read: Romans 10:9-11

A beautiful lesson about the church is given by Paul in First Corinthians. He tells us that cooperation is essential. No one person is to control or try to take care of all God's Work, himself or herself. One person lives the Christian life, telling others about Jesus Christ (plants) another teaches or disciples that person in teaching him or her God's Word (waters) but only God can give the increase or we would say only God can convict and draw people to Him. In a group of worshipers (we call this our church) competition is never right. When people begin competing, self steps in for the glory of what is being done. There is enormous potential in a group of people, but it will never be realized if everyone's objective is to take credit for the results. Paul uses the image of metal being purified by a refining fire.

When we stand before Jesus Christ, only those works, minus the impurities, will be left. Let us imagine the things that will remain pure as gold and silver. They can be: Acts of charity, kindness, truth, humility, fair play, keeping our word and trusting God to keep His promises and working in the place God has given us for His glory, not for compliments or popularity. The things called hay, wood and stubble which will burn up are any abuses we have heaped on someone, lies we have told, selfishness, turning a deaf ear to the needy, trying to lock ourselves into power and lock others out, working for God for the wrong reasons, and lack of faith in the one who gave His life so each person on earth would have a choice to accept Him.

Read: 1st Corinthians 3:9-15

*A*re we guilty of going to the Lord's House on Sunday and having a form of worship for the one day of the week and forgetting Him the rest of the week? This is not to be the way of a Christian. Many times we see people come to the Lord, ask forgiveness , we call them new converts, and they go out without any further help or encouragement from the other members of the congregation. This was not true in Peter's time. Of course, society was altogether different then, and the new converts would stay with the apostles. When we study, we see this was necessary, because they had no weekly jobs, etc. Today, what should we do for a new Christian? First, they need to be taught. We should take time to talk with them, teach them, and above all they need encouragement. Do you notice when a person is discouraged, or we would say "down and out?"

We. as older and more mature Christians, should observe others. Sometimes a person needs a hug and they need to hear you and me say, "I am praying for you, or is there something I can do to help?" If we have no love one for another we do not have Jesus Christ, or we have not gotten out of the "baby stage" as a Christian. The Bible tells us of the wonderful love, compassion and forgiveness of Jesus Christ and He is the one who is to be our example. We should follow Him, always. A few years ago there was a bracelet that had WWJD on it and these were popular, but did people really take the meaning to heart for everyday living?The apostles took the teachings to heart and were beaten because they did.

Read: Acts 5:40-42

$\mathcal{P}$ersistence is a word we hear very little about. When we think of prayer, how persistent are we? Do we petition God once for something or someone and then think it is no need to pray for that person or thing again. Do we "give up"? We are never taught to give up on God. Let us think of Jesus' life and all the disappointments He encountered when dealing with humanity. When He asked the disciples to watch and pray with Him in the Garden, and came back to find them sleeping, not once, but three times, did He sit down and give up? No, Jesus saw the weakness of all human flesh and He knew that was the reason for His birth, and His life and He also knew their sins were the reason He should shed His Blood. This is the reason the Bible tells us to pray without ceasing.

God is telling us He will answer our prayers and we are to be persistent. He will not always answer with "yes" quickly as we expect, because He knows what we need and when we need it. There are times we ask for things we do not need with motives that are not right and God knows the heart. The answer might be "no" or "not until you are able to handle what you are asking for in the right way." Faith in Jesus Christ is the answer. When we pray we must have faith to believe that He will answer our prayers, according to His Will and Purpose. We find one in the Bible who had so much faith she just knew if she could touch the hem of Jesus' garment, she would be healed. She believed so strongly she fought the crowds to get to Jesus and her petition was granted, and another who pled for her daughter to be healed.

Read: Matthew 15:21-28

*W*e look at the news and see very little about the small towns, but they are a vital part of society, also. When we look into the Scriptures we find a small town that is very important and that town is Nazareth. This is a community that we would say was "across the tracks". God chose this place where Jesus would grow up and invest the most years of His life. This tells us, once again, that God cares for everyone, the cities and the small neighborhoods. Maybe you live in a small community or came from a small town and always thought you did not count because of the circumstances of your growing-up years. This is not true in God's eyes because Jesus came for each individual. Each soul is precious to Him. How do I know this? Look at His life and you will see He ministered to all peoples, the rich, poor, lame, blind and unbelievers. He came to save everyone, if he or she will only accept His Love and forgiveness.

We find that Nazareth chose to reject Jesus. This reveals to us that people of all walks of life have rejected Jesus' message, but some have listened and believed. The question was asked, "Can anything good come out of Nazareth?" (John 1:46) Nathanael's answer was "come and see." Our answer is a definite "YES, The most wonderful gift ever known to man."

Read: Luke 4:16-21 & 28-30

$\mathcal{N}$o matter who we are or what we do for a living, we are bound to face struggles in this life. These struggles can be a number of circumstances as job loss, injury, illness, emotional pain, financial pressures and death of loved ones. One of Job's friends, Eliphaz noted, "Man is born to trouble as the sparks fly upward"(Job 5:7) When trouble comes, people often want to blame God and this should not even come into the mind of a Christian. Some struggles, we bring on ourselves and others are brought on by Satanic forces. It is often hard to convince people of the power of spiritual warfare in this day and age. Secular thinking dismisses all talk of the supernatural realm, saying it is superstition left over from the ancient world. We are to study God's Word which teaches that evil forces exist and have substantial influence on the world and human events. We find Paul calling them "principalities." This word is used in Romans 8:38, where even angels will separate you from God are fallen angels. Also rulers are mentioned aspowers and principalities are all evil forces.

There are times when evil forces are present and we can see Satan at work and at other times Satan and his forces have other ways (undercover) to capture people away from God. There are many belief systems taught today, to influence people, many in authority (leaders) teaching the wrong doctrine and belief. We need to study God's word so we will not be ignorant when we face these wiles of Satan.

Read: Ephesians 6:12-17

When we think of and study about the past, we see fathers, mothers, sons and daughters who received promises from God. Does this tell us God still gives promises to us? Yes, there are many promises given God's children and you will find them in the Bible. God promised Abraham and Sarah a son and we see this happening, even in extreme old age. In Isaiah 55:6 God promises mercy and pardon. Jesus was promised to all people in Isaiah 53, and He came when the time was right. He was rejected by most people, but shed His blood so that all who would come to Him might be saved. This is the salvation God promised Judah as his father Jacob(Israel) bless him in the last Chapter of Genesis 49:10.

Jesus was born from the seed of Judah. Jesus promised His people a Comforter after He was gone away and we find the Holy Spirit descending on the day of Pentecost Jesus made a promise we need to remember, daily. That promise is in the scripture reading below.

Read: John 14:1-3

We see the disciple John as the "apostle of love" because of the frequent use of that theme in his writings and because the Gospel of John refers to him as the disciple whom Jesus loved. He certainly did not start out as a model of charity. We see Jesus calling John and his brother the sons of thunder Would this mean they were loud, opinionated and headstrong? When we look at different lives who followed Jesus we see the human faults and yet Jesus loved them. We see selfishness and a longing for popularity or I might say glory when these brothers asked if they could sit on Jesus' right and left hand in His kingdom. These would be the best and highest seats, and the other disciples resented the request.

On another occasion they suggested calling down fire on a Samaritan village and were rebuked by Jesus. We see John's exposure to Jesus bringing an amazing change in his life. This did not happen suddenly, but listening to Jesus' teaching and seeing the love He had for everyone opened his eyes and he learned about the love of Christ. After Jesus ascended, we see John who had wanted to destroy the Samaritans going with Peter to preach to them. How the Love of Jesus Christ works to change a person's actions and thinking! Have you asked Him to change your way of thinking and acting? Jesus let the brothers know they would suffer for Him, but He did not grant their request for the highest seats.

Read: Mark 10:35-40

$\mathcal{D}$o you have a leadership role in your community or church? Jesus shows that Biblical leadership begins with humility by serving others. Yet, we have those, today, who seek leadership roles by masking their true intentions. They will manipulate people to attain their selfish ambitions. This happens in our Churches and in our Government, also. There is no real concern for others, except to use them to achieve their ambitions. Why do we desire greatness? We want to be good or great in our job, or a great scholar. Seeking to attain excellence is not wrong, except when we seek it for the wrong reasons.

The Lord challenged the motives of His followers rather than their desires. Jesus knew there were those who wanted power to lord it over others, seeking position and power for means to personal gain, not service to others. When there was a dispute among the disciples as to which of them would be greatest, and Jesus knowing this said, " he that is greatest among you, is he that serves." We see Jesus teaching humility by washing the feet of the disciples, which was only done by servants during that day. We should search our hearts today. Why do we serve? Are we serving because we love God and others?

Read: Matt: 20:27 & 28 and John 13:3-5

$\mathcal{A}$ person of faith has never been promised an easy life but the promise they have is a Savior who will be with them "through it all." He will walk with us each day, giving us the strength we need for the day. A person of faith will face many misunderstandings and challenges to his or her values and sometimes outright opposition. There will be times you might feel as though you are swimming against the tide. This is nothing new, because we see the new believers in the Book of Acts felt the stress of opposition, also. They encountered arrest of their leaders, rage and many plots against them.

How did they respond to these things? They prayed together, gathering together regularly for spiritual refueling. Jesus told us He would send the Comforter to us and we have the Holy Spirit with us through each day, after we accept Jesus as Savior and Lord. Let us not forget to pray with and for our friends and loved ones. Just as they needed each other in Acts, we need each other today. Have you prayed for someone today, offered a word of encouragement or comfort?

Read: Acts 4:18-22

After Mary has been visited by the Holy Spirit and knows she is to have a Child, a holy Child, she goes to visit her cousin, Elizabeth, who is also expecting a child destined to be the forerunner of Jesus Christ. When we say forerunner it is as though we are looking at a person as he or she races through growth clearing the way for the next runner. This would be the right way to envision John the Baptist. He preached preparing the people for a Messiah. I want to think of John as a person sent ahead to make a path for those who would follow, as a person walking through a brush filled path. Maybe cutting a large bush that would keep another person from staying on the right path.

As Mary visits her cousin Elizabeth she actually gave a message or some people call this "Mary's song. We find in the song she praises God, her Savior for the great things He has done, for His Mercy, strength, for filling the hungry with good things. I want to think of a person away from God, searching, but never satisfied, spiritually hungry for something more in their lives When he or she accepts Jesus, that hunger is filled. God promised Abraham, hundreds of years before we see Mary's visit, He would establish an everlasting covenant with Isaac, his son and with his seed after him. In Genesis Chapter 49:10, Jacob (Israel) is blessing Judah, promising him the sceptre would not pass from him, until Jesus came. Nathan gave David, a descendant of Judah, the message that His house would be established forever. God kept His promise, as He always does, using Mary to give birth to Jesus, who came to earth to die, shedding His Blood for our sins.

Read: Luke 1:46-55

*T*here will be times in your life when you will be laughed at, ridiculed and called many names because you believe in and serve God. We must not think this is a rare thing. Jesus was called names by those who were the religious leaders of His day. I did not say they were Christians but "religious". There are many who are religious, but do not believe in Jesus Christ, the Savior of the World. They serve other Gods. Jesus was called illegitimate (John 8: 41) and many other names. They even called Him demonic and a Samaritan (called the lowest class of people).

We know Jesus is our example, so let us look and see how we are to handle adversity in this life. First, if you have accepted Jesus, asked Him to forgive you of your sins and turned from your old way of living, you have a Savior who will always walk beside you. How do I know He is always with me? Because when He went away, His promise was, "I will send a comforter to you." He never promised to take away all our troubles, but He did promise to walk with us. We must remember God never breaks a promise, so we know we have the presence of the Holy Spirit. Jesus never gave up on us and we are to keep serving Him, no matter how much people reject us, call us names or shun us.

Read: John 8:42-47

*T*oday, let us think about honoring God with all we do. When we open our eyes in the morning, no matter what causes us to wake up, we are blessed by God to see another day. How are we going to use this day? In those early moments of the day, what goes through your mind? Do you think of all the things you have to do during the day or do you thank God for allowing you another day? Did you ever realize that you and the sun share a reason for rising? The reason is to share the Glory of God. If we belong to God, we are to display the Glory of the risen Christ who lives in you!

The sun warms the earth, but do we radiate the warmth of God's Love? We are not saved by the Blood of Jesus, to hide the Glory and Love of God, but we are to be living witnesses of His Love for us. First, we need to study God's Word, so we will know how to show His Love to others. Next, we are to realize that everything we do falls into the category of showcasing, not ourselves, but God. We are not to hide our love for God under a bushel, but allow others to see and know He lives in us. We are to witness for Him, not just with talk, but we are to walk with Him, showing His Love, daily. At the end of the day, we each should stop and ask ourselves, "Have I honored God, today?"

Read: 2nd Corinthians 4:6 & 7

Do you seek maturity as a Christian? When a person accepts Christ as Savior and Lord, a new journey begins. Just like a plant that draws its strength from the ground we need nurturing with the right foods. You might ask, "what are those foods I need to grow"? The answer is Study of God's Word and Prayer. When we study the Bible it is God speaking to us. We might say teaching us, and when we pray we are talking to Him. He gives us the strength and wisdom to live each day for Him and we grow from a "babe" in Christ to a more mature stage, gradually. Another question we might ask is this: "Do I ever reach full maturity?" We will become fully mature when we reach Heaven.

In First Corinthians 13:12, we are told this: "now we see through a glass, darkly; but then face to face; now I know in part; but then I shall know even as also I am known." This tells me I only know a part of the things God has for us, but then everything will be complete. To grow and blossom, as a Christian, we must reach toward Jesus Christ, the Son as a plant reaches toward the sun for growth.

Read: John 15:5 & 6

During our lives we will have sickness and sorrow. We might be so sick we cannot put one foot before the other and we just want to give us or as we said in times past, "crawl into a hole and die." You might have a few days when you cannot function physically, as usual, but this should not keep you from worshiping the King of King. Satan would have a person give us at the first trouble, but God wants us to persevere. You might say, "But I have lost my loved one, the one I have depended on and I don't know what to do." The answer is this: Ask God to give you the strength to stand, to keep serving Him, to walk with you through it all.

Do you remember the song we sing "through it all." In this song the words are penned, "through it all I learned to trust in God," "I learned to depend upon His Word". We, as Christians, have a Comforter and we know God will hear us when we pray to Him, asking Him for strength. A Christian should never become bitter when bad things happen in this life. We should not say, "why me?" Others have had the same troubles, and we could say, "why not me?" The best thought a Christian can have is this: "God is not through with me, yet." "He has more for me to do" and when my work on earth is finished, He will call me to a home in Heaven to be with Him. Sure, our strength can fail, we might become weary, but our faith will sustain us, when we take the next step.

Read: Isaiah 40:29-31

*I*n all God has told us in His Word, He makes one thing very clear: He loves each person. Have you been in a group of people and no-one there knew you? You felt as though your were faceless, alone with no friends. This is not true with God. He knows each individual by name, as our friends know us by name. But there is more, and that is the fact that God knows every detail about each of us. The beautiful thought is this: He cares about every facet of your life and my life.

If you know Jesus Christ as your Savior and Lord, and I pray you do, he is waiting to hear from you, today. Jesus is a friend like no other and He will walk with us though all our troubled times, lead and guide us when we make decisions. But we must remember He forces His will on no person. If you have never received Him and asked Him to forgive your sins, Jesus is waiting for you to invite Him into your heart and become the main part of your life. Jesus came to earth, leaving His heavenly home, lived among people, and died on a cross so that each person would have the same chance to be saved eternally. He gave a free gift, but it is up to the individual to accept this gift of salvation.

Psalm 139:1-4 and 14

When a person first accepts Jesus Christ as Savior and Lord, he or she wants to know all about Him and all the things He did and said. That person needs someone to come along side them and encourage them in the Word of God. We miss the mark many times in our churches. A person is converted and left on their own with no older Christian to help them, no person will step up to the plate and say, "please call me anytime" or "let's meet and have Bible study". In this society we have become too busy to do the work God intends us to do. When we look at the New Testament, we see Barnabas going with Saul (converted to be Paul), to other older followers of Christ. Have you heard the remark, "well, he or she might say they are changed, but I will not believe it." The person they are talking of is the very person who has lived away from God in the past, and this person has accepted Jesus Christ as Savior. They need help to grow, because at the time they are a "babe" in Christ.

A growing process has to take place if they are to be of use to God in the future. Also, we need to look at our lives, as Christians, and ask, "am I as close to God as I was, once?" We, who have been Christians for a long time, have a tendency to grow cold. We do not pray as we once did, we do not study God's Word as we did before. When we become too busy for these things, the only thing we should say is this: "I am too busy with things that have no eternal value." How thankful are we to God for sending Jesus to this earth so we could become adopted into the family of God and become joint heirs with Christ?

Read: 1st Chronicles 16:8-12

You and I have been blind-sided by Satan, many times in our lives. I am talking about the time or times when we are very peaceful and all of a sudden an attack comes. It can be an accident, an illness, death, or many other things that will knock us to our knees. Do we know what to do, or do we feel that we have been knocked down, deserted by God, and do we just want to go to bed and cover our heads and whimper? None of the above will give you the solace you need, but there is One who is waiting for you to call out to Him. Tell Jesus about your needs, sure He knows, but He is waiting for us to ask Him for His help and the strength we need.

Above all, do not let Satan get victory in your trouble. Do not become bitter, but just remember to trust in God, take Him at His Word and know He cares for you and will sustain you. If we "give up" or have a "pity party" we will be no good for the work God has given us. A good Christian, with a number of illnesses, made a statement I have though of more than once. He said, "We are not to say, why me? but other people have troubles and we are to say why not me? " We have times of testing and if we continue to depend upon God these times will make us stronger Christians. At the end of life, Lord, help me to say, "I have fought a good fight." "I have kept the faith."

Read: 1st Timothy 4:7 & 8

We see a little girl look at the father she adores. In her eyes, he is the most handsome man in the world and can do anything. In fact, she thinks he is perfect and she will call on him when she needs something. This is the way we should fix our eyes on God. We should pray like this: "I do not want to turn my eyes from you, O God, I want them to stay on you, no matter what happens in my life". We should have the same unblinking stare toward God, the child has toward her earthly dad.

Do we wait for a time of trouble to look toward God, to call out to Him? Why not look to Him in adoration, thanking Him for all good and perfect gifts that are given us? Do we wait until we are in trouble to realize the only safe place to go is to God? We have His promises and when we think of fixing our eyes on Him, we need to realize He has His gaze fixed on us too. Psalm 139: 2, tells us He knows our downsitting and our uprising and understands our thoughts afar off. Let us renew our determination to stay fixed on God, despite all the distractions of everyday life.

Read: Isaiah 26:3 & 4

*D*o you remember the old west shows we saw many times and the greed for gold? People have a tendency to seek for earthly treasures, but they will never satisfy. Do you have the popular "bucket list" which is filled with all the things you want to do before you die? There are those who are rushing to do all these things because they are afraid they will not have time to get them done in this life. None of this will bring peace and satisfaction to the human soul. Even though a person might have money, take many vacations and have all the earthly thrills, they will continue to have an empty place inside. There will be a need that is unfulfilled.

This morning I am able to recommend a way to fill that void in your life. There is a treasure map with a guarantee and that map guarantees your finding the greatest treasure of all, a treasure that will satisfy everyone and the searching will be over. That treasure map is available and waiting to be discovered by you. The treasure map is found in God's Word, the treasure, God Himself, He will be your God for the asking. There is no other such a friend as He. Have you found this perfect Treasure called salvation? If you have not, why not pick up His Word and ask Him to fill that deep longing in your heart? This treasure is big enough for everyone.

Read: Matthew 7:7-11

*W*hen we think of the Love of Jesus, we should all bow our heads and thank Him over and over. He left a beautiful, heavenly home to come to this earth and live in a very poor environment. Yes, He could have chosen a rich household, but when we think of riches, we see what they do to people and there would have been no virgin with the right selfless attitude among the rich people of the day. God chose an innocent young virgin who had probably known many hardships in her short life and had learned to depend upon God. During this time of year we think of gifts for the Christmas Season. Is the general idea this? "That person gave me a gift and it was valued at so much, so I need to give one that will cost the same" or "If I do not give them a gift, he or she will be angry" or "I wanted something more than I received."

There are many who have forgotten the joy of this season and are only thinking of material things. Let us not be guilty of such actions or thoughts, as Christians. Jesus took on the form of a servant, even washing His disciples' feet. He never asked for gifts and He gave freely. Did you know we are responsible for giving the entire year. First, the tithe belongs to God and is not a gift. Next, there are many who need some of our time, we need to share God's Word with others and there are numerous other needs. Look around, become aware of the places you might be able to give, expecting nothing in return, but getting the greater blessing when you help someone. Always remember Jesus gave the greatest gift ever given when He went to the cross for you and me.

Read: John 15:13

*I*n Bible Study we see Jesus healing lepers. When the ten were healed only one came back to thank Him. a leper is someone who has a dreaded disease which begins very small. For instance, this disease can begin on the end of a finger or tip of the nose or toe. This is the way evil begins in a person's life. If Satan came onto a Christian suddenly tempting him or her with wrong doing, they would recognize it and turn away. Sin has a way of creeping upon a person and Satan has ways of using people to tempt other people to get them involved in sinful things. "Try this, it will make your life happy" or "just this once to be with the crowd", and sin grows until it takes over the person. Just like a person with leprosy there is no cure but God's grace. We find Paul writing to the Church in Corinth about trying to hide, ignore or cover up sin within the fellowship. Hypocrisy within the Church will effect the entire congregation, and Paul told the people to face up to this and root it out of the church.

You might ask, "how will my sin effect others?" There is always someone watching you and they might say, "this person is a Christian and if he or she does this, it is ok." Influence is so important in our Christian walk. Of course, we know, we are not perfect, but let us ask God to help us walk daily in His will. We must remember there is no hiding from God. He sees our actions and knows our thoughts.

Read: 1st Corinthians 5:1-6

*H*ow do you feel when you ask a person, "how are you?' and you get a long story of sickness and trouble from that person? You do not feel lifted up by this person because of the negative mind-set. It is important for a Christian to think on the blessings God gives us each day. When we begin counting there is no end. We are not to look at others and criticize but say, "Thank you Jesus, but by your Grace, there go I, please help that person in their troubles." How different is the feeling you get when a person responds to your, "how are you", with a cheerful outlook. Even though you might know they have troubles, their faith is steadfast and you see in the midst of their trouble they have the ability to smile and lift other people up. These are the kinds of Christian needed in this world. With the right outlook and our eyes fixed on Jesus and His goodness, we will be able to bring warmth and light to all those we meet.

When we see how God has been so merciful to us, we should praise Him. Did you ever think of Christians being the richest people on earth? We are joint-heirs with Jesus Christ and will inherit a home that is so beautiful our minds cannot comprehend the beauty. Even though we read about Heaven, we, as Paul say are looking through a mirror darkly, but one day we will see and know it all, clearly. Be happy, if you belong to Jesus Christ, you have many blessings ahead If you do not belong to Him, please accept the free gift He came to earth to give you.

Read: Psalm 62:5-8

I want to wish everyone a wonderful, blessed Christmas. Let us remember this is Jesus' Birthday and thank Him for all His goodness to us. The world needed a perfect Person to go to God for our forgiveness, our salvation and Jesus was the only one who was perfect. Our minds have a hard time comprehending John 1:1&2 but we should all keep this Scripture in our hearts. The world was awaiting a king, because of the prophecy in the Old Testament. As human beings will do, they were looking for a rich king who would come to earth and immediately set up a kingdom. They did not understand a king being born in a lowly manger among the cattle. This was not what the people expected. He was to come in the glory of Majesty and take over the earth. This will happen in the last days, but human beings do not realize God's timing is not the same as time is to us.

The Scripture tells us a thousand years is as a day to God. Jesus will set up His kingdom when he returns to earth. Jesus walked among men, healed, preached, raised the dead and did many wonderful works, but the world did not accept Him. He was born to die for our sins. This was God's plan and He went to the cross and laid down His life willingly, shedding his Blood for you and me. The prediction of His coming was hundreds of years before He came.

Read: Isaiah 53:2-7

God bless each person reading this on Christmas Day! We should think of the Love of God. The song says, "The Love of God, how rich and Pure" and it also says, "It will forever endure." True words written to worship the wonderful Son of God who came to earth for you and me. He could have roared from the top of a mountain, yet He whispered in the voice of a Baby. He could have ordered each of us to obey Him, but He wants us to love Him and freely give our hearts to Him.

We must remember we exist because God allows us to live on this earth, and instead of ordering us to serve Him, He woos us to love Him. When we think of His eyes, we will see them brimming with love. God wants each of us to choose Him today, that's how much He loves us. His love is free, and His forgiveness is yours for the asking. If you do not know Jesus, the Son of God, ask Him into your heart today. No Love is more beautiful than the love of Jesus, who left Heaven to dwell on earth and die for you and me.

Read: Psalm 18:1-3

$\mathcal{A}$re you thankful, this morning, or do you have a "let down" feeling because all the excitement of Christmas is over for you? This should not be. The gift of Jesus is an eternal gift. We, as Christians, are able to keep the beautiful story of His birth in our hearts all year. As the song tells us, "let's get excited and go tell everybody that Jesus Christ is Lord." Reading of the life of Laura Ingalls Wilder, we see a child so very happy to have in her stocking a cup, stick of candy and a penny. Today, we have become so materially minded, we think too much of "what I want." Jesus was left out of the celebration by many, but it was His Birthday! What small important riches have you been given. When we begin thinking on this, we see we have been given wonderful riches. Family love, one for another, is cherished, but the greatest, and richest gift of all is the love of Jesus.

There are memories in the past years that would seem as small at the penny gift to others, but these times are most precious to us, because we know they were gifts from God. Instead of thinking in the negative, let us look forward to another day to talk to Jesus, to read His Word, to think on all He has done for us, and be happy!

Read: Matthew 7:7 & 8

*I*sn't it wonderful that we can have a God of all comfort? Everything might be in our favor for a period of time, all our bills are paid, we are in good health, we have a great job and we feel we are in favor with God. However, there might come a time when all aspects of life seem to crash down around us an we find ourselves in desperate need of the comfort of God. No problem or heartache is outside of God's range of comfort. He has unlimited resources, a vast wellspring at His disposal at all times

There are many names for God mentioned in the Bible and each name has a specific meaning. When we see the Word Adonai we know the meaning is Lord or Master. We hear God telling Moses to tell the people "I am" and we know He has been forever God, We see the word Jehovah Jireh and we know this meaning is "my provider". When God is our Lord and Master we may go to Him for comfort at any time and we also know He will provide for us a beautiful heavenly home when we die.

Read: 2nd Corinthians 1:3 & 4 and John 14:27

*T*his is the day the Lord hath made, let us rejoice and be glad in it! God gives us each day and if we are not careful, we will take the blessings in this life for granted. In other words, we will just go along and forget to thank God. On this day, think of the many blessings you have been given the past week. If you had a troubled time, God is a present help in time of trouble. How blessed we are to have the freedom to serve Him. Do not squander this great privilege.

There are many people in the world who will have to hide and worship God today because of persecution. When we think of the Holy Land and our tour there and remember the sign of the fish over doors and how people had to worship in upper rooms so there could be a "look-out" for soldiers and government officials who would arrest those worshiping Jesus, we should bow our heads and thank God we live in a free Country. Yes, we see some of our freedom taken away and we should always be alert and stand for God and our Country. Go to the Church of your choice today and worship the Lord of Lord, King of Kings, Jesus Christ. He loves you and wants to commune with you.

Read: Psalm 105:1-5

As we study the Book of Exodus and see the calling of Moses, we see excuses made to get away from God's plan. Moses used the excuse of people who would not hear him or believe God sent him. When God gave him signs he could use to prove he was sent by God, he then used the excuse of not being eloquent of speech (today we might hear this, "I am not able to speak in public") but God told him He would teach Him. Then we hear the use of the excuse we hear many times, "let someone else do it." God does not accept excuses from us when we refuse to serve Him. We might use this, "I just do not have the time." Each person is given the same amount of hours in a day.

God does not call each person to lead as He called Moses, but there are many ways to serve Him. If we belong to Him, we are to follow the nudges we get to do this or that for His glory. He calls each of us to live a Christian Life, daily. We should not have to tell a person, "I am a Christian," because our life should show in whom we believe. Let us not forget this: others listen as we talk, but they watch our daily walk. This includes our language, our honesty, our forgiveness, and our attitude toward others.

Read: John 15:7-10

*H*ow difficult it is for a human being to figure out or we might say understand the Grace of God. We read of a person like John Newton, the author of the hymn, "Amazing Grace". He said, " I was a blasphemer, an apostate and an infidel." He was a former slave trader and states, "I was capable of anything and I had no fear of God." Swearing was a habit that was deeply rooted in his nature. But when he called out to God he was saved. We look at this way of living and we are so disgusted with such an evil lifestyle and we might ask, "Why did God pour out His Grace on such a man?" The answer is, "Because He loved even this vile man."

We might look at Saul in the Book of Acts and say the same thing, but we have the record of him being changed. God even changed his name to Paul and he became a great Missionary. God loves each person and He loves you. Nothing you might have done in the past is so bad that you are beyond the reach of the Grace of God. God's Grace is nothing short of a miracle and we cannot figure it out, but this free gift is waiting for you to accept it.

Read: Ephesians 2:8 & 9

*Y*esterday we talked about the Grace of God and how He has forgiven and used those who were in the mire of sin and totally against Him. How are we at forgiving? When someone hurts our feelings, how do we react? Would it not be better to endure that smart which nobody feels but us, than to commit a hasty action and hurt others around us? God bids us do good for evil. He has promised He will work all things out (even the bad things) for our good. When we rely on this promise God will give us the strength to forgive and return good for evil to those who have hurt us.

There are those who think a forgiving person is a coward, but the opposite is true. The only way we are able to forgive and do good for evil is to rely on the strength of God. This tells me it takes a strong person to forgive and that strength has to come from calling upon God. When we look at this, we say, "This is not fair," but this is "God Honoring," and that's what matters. We do not know of a person more poorly treated than Joseph was by his brothers.

I pray that each of you have a happy and properous New Year!

Read: Genesis 50:14-21

Made in the USA
Charleston, SC
23 November 2016